How to Deal with
Low
Self-esteem

How to Deal with
Low Self-esteem

Christine Wilding

JOHN
MURRAY
LEARNING

Also available in ebook

For Oliver and Tom, Poppy and Lola, with love as always

Contents

Introduction

As a psychotherapist, I work on a daily basis with people who suffer from low self-esteem. These people may present to me with a variety of different problems, ranging from chronic depression to seeing their lives fall apart after a job loss, bereavement or other trauma. The problems may differ but the common factor is that people are often unable to deal successfully with these issues because of their lack of confidence in their ability to do so. As a therapist, my role is not to resolve my clients' personal crises but rather to build their self-esteem and resilience so that they can then resolve their own problems, however diverse and difficult these may be. The purpose of this book is to offer the same professional help towards building strong self-esteem in an easy-format, self-help way that will enable a wider audience to benefit from the standard of help that therapists regularly give to their clients.

You may already have heard of cognitive behavioural therapy (CBT) and this is the therapeutic approach we will be using. CBT is a therapy that focuses on resolving practical problems in the 'here and now'. We only go back into the past if it is important and relevant to present-day beliefs and actions. In the main, we are working with you to discover exactly what your difficulties are now, to understand what maintains them and then to find solutions to overcome them. CBT is very interested in your thinking about your problems, checking to see if you fall into one of the many negative thinking traps. It is also curious about your behaviours in relation to your difficulties – is what you are doing making things better, maintaining the problem or possibly making it worse? CBT shows you how to restructure both how you think and what you do in order to get the outcome you would like.

To give structure to the book and to help you to feel fully supported as you work through it, it is divided into five sections, each building on the previous section. You might find it best to look through the whole book first, to get your bearings and to give yourself an idea of what to expect, and then go back to the beginning and work through it slowly. Don't move forward until you feel that you have both really understood what is being suggested and undertaken the tasks that you will find in the text.

CBT bases its help on what we call 'guided discovery'. Put simply, if how you think, feel and behave now keeps your self-esteem low and other problems activated, we are interested in discovering what would happen if you changed things – tried something new or thought about things differently perhaps. You won't be asked to take on random ideas, which is why we call this discovery 'guided'; you will be helped and supported by a safe structure which, although it takes you, necessarily, out of your comfort zone, will also help you to tolerate rather than fear the possibility of failure (which, in most cases, may not happen). You will be helped towards having a greater awareness of your thoughts, feelings and consequent actions. The tasks in the book will be based on this – on getting you to look at things differently and do things differently and then weigh up what you have discovered from these efforts, which will hopefully build up your confidence.

About this book

This book features the **STEP P**ast method for overcoming low self-esteem. **STEP P**ast is a five-step approach, drawing on cognitive behavioural therapy techniques, to give practical and emotional support to anyone affected by self-esteem issues.

S – Support helps you come to terms with the problem, and maps out the road to recovery.

T – Tackle the negative thoughts and behaviour patterns that hold you back.

E – Escape the behaviours and situations that make your life a struggle.

P – Practice provides coping strategies, showing you how to adjust your responses and replace harmful thoughts, when they occur.

P – Progress to a healthier, happier new life – without fear of setbacks or relapse.

In Part 1 of *How to Deal with Low Self-esteem*, Support, you will learn more about self-esteem and gain confidence in your ability to turn it from low to high. As CBT is a very structured therapy we shall also work together to set some goals for you. It is important to do this early so that you have an idea of what you would like to achieve and feel supported in your efforts. You will also learn more about what may be keeping your self-esteem low at present so that you can begin to identify why your own efforts to escape the low self-esteem trap are not yet working.

Part 2, Tackle, will help you learn about the tools that are available to promote change and will be helped to see how they might work for you. You will be introduced to CBT in more detail and make a start in gaining confidence. You will also be invited to learn something of mindful awareness which, if you wish to incorporate this into your practice, will add enormously to your emerging self-confidence and peace of mind.

Part 3, Escape, will show you how to break free from your difficulties, using both the basic tools you have learned and also developing wider skills to increase your confidence.

In Part 4, Practice, you will learn how to increase your self-esteem in specific situations, such as social situations and close relationships.

Part 5, Progress, will help you to continue your progress towards excellent self-esteem. In addition, there are appendices dealing with specific problems that can hold people back but which are not specifically covered in the main part of this book.

Keeping notes

Make notes as you read. Whether you use pen and paper or an electronic device such as a smartphone or tablet, the important thing is that your notes are easily accessible and meaningful when you look back at what you have written. Jot down anything that particularly strikes you to think about further or to practise, as well as doing the tasks that begin 'Write down ...'. If using pen and paper, it might be a good idea to have a dedicated notebook or folder for your notes so that shopping lists. phone messages, etc. don't get mixed up with the valuable work you are doing.

PART 1

Support

Understand where you are now and where you want to be

CHAPTER 1

Understanding what self-esteem is

Overview

In this chapter you will learn:

- the role that negative beliefs play in maintaining low self-esteem
- the role these faulty beliefs play in preventing you from overcoming it.

For example, a person with an 'I am worthless' belief may need to chip away at the fact that being bullied at school made them feel worthless. Someone else may have the same belief but caused by the rejection of someone they loved. CBT will help you to question the authority of these beliefs in a variety of different ways.

What does self-esteem mean to you?

Up to now, not feeling as good about yourself as you would like may have seemed a bit of a puzzle, or you may have recognized that you have low self-esteem but not known how this had come about or what to do about it. To overcome it, you need to understand *why* you struggle with it. This will offer insights that will help you as you learn new structures to support good self-esteem You will develop your own self-esteem profile, so that in later chapters of the book you can work on areas that are personal to you. Learning what maintains low self-esteem will give you the foundation for personal change that further chapters in this book will develop with you.

Some people with low self-esteem don't even recognize that they are suffering from it. They see their negative self-image as facts and truths rather than just a way of seeing themselves. Yet believing something with all your heart and soul doesn't necessarily make it true: it is simply a negative thought, which this therapy can teach you to examine and view in a more balanced way that will make you feel better about yourself.

If you had good self-esteem, how would you know? How would you feel? For most people, good self-esteem involves the ability to think of ourselves as 'OK' and to believe that others think we are OK as well. It also involves not being too hard on ourselves (or thinking that others are being hard on us) when we say or do things that are not OK. A specific example might be having a positive attitude to life's ups and downs, which means not automatically expecting the worst to happen (activated perhaps by a 'bad things always happen to me' belief), and also believing that if things do go wrong, you will cope with the adversity in the best way you can, accepting that life isn't fair all the time.

This style of thinking and behaviour allows you to take managed risks, making it easier to discover (and feel) the joys of success. It gives you the ability to make difficult decisions, as you feel confident that things will probably go well but that you can cope if they don't.

What would help you to feel better about yourself? You may have some personal views, for example:

- being able to get on well with my colleagues at work
- having a good relationship with my children
- getting into the club tennis team.

One thing we know is that what drives our self-esteem is different for all of us, so although we have talked above about the well-known, all round traits that embrace good self-esteem, everyone has their own view of what would make a big difference to them. These views, however, can fall flat when we do achieve something yet find that we feel no better about ourselves. The skill of 'guided discovery' will help you towards identifying what is really going on for you and what will really make positive changes.

Your Inner Critic

The architect of low self-esteem is our 'Inner Critic', whose job it is to constantly whisper in our ear, reminding us of our faults and weaknesses. Use your imagination to imagine what your Inner Critic looks like. What about a pantomime character – tall and thin in an ill-fitting suit and a huge top hat? Or a little gremlin that sits on your shoulder chattering away to you. Or perhaps an animal, or a radio you can't switch off? You might even want to give your Inner Critic a name.

Try the exercise below. Using imagery in this way will help you to view your critical self as something, or someone, external to yourself that you don't need to keep listening to. In turn, it will be much easier for you to fight something you can visualize and whom you can tell to 'get lost' as your self-esteem improves.

Behaviour changing strategy

Task

Conjure up a description of your Inner Critic. Make it as colourful as you can. The more you bring imagery into play here, the easier it will be for you to deal with your Inner Critic. Make the caricature humorous, which will also be helpful.

We call this 'externalizing' and it encourages you to see your negative thoughts and beliefs as something external to your rational, more balanced thinking, the thinking that you would apply to normal problem-solving, for example.

Now replay in your mind the last critical comment it made. Does imagining your Inner Critic in this way help you to loosen the extent to which you believe the criticism?

Once settled in, your Inner Critic is very hard to dislodge. We learn to live with it, and trust and believe what it says. One of the main goals of this book is to enable you to remove your Inner Critic and see it for the fraud that it is. With a little work, this is achievable, and you will be amazed at how differently you will view yourself without your Inner Critic constantly demoralizing you.

Mistaken 'certainties'

Low self-esteem can be caused by a succession of failures for which we blame ourselves, or by a chronic 'drip, drip' of being told that we're not up to much (or perceiving comments as critical even when this may not have been the case). We tend not to see these perceptions as possibilities but as certainties.

Take a moment to think about your view of your own low self-esteem. Is it generalized? Have you always felt this way, or can you point to a specific time, period or event in your life when you first lost your natural self-confidence? You might identify:

- a time frame, e.g. two years ago
- an event, e.g. when a relationship broke up
- a period in your life, e.g. when I went to university.

The answer to this question will help you to identify whether your problem is:

- **unhelpful thinking:** that is, you have taken a negative view of events that have befallen you and incorporated these thoughts into your day-to-day thinking style. For example, you have always thought of yourself as attractive until someone you care for deeply ends a relationship, when you decide you must be unlikeable; or you always considered yourself intelligent until you failed an exam, when you realized that you were not so smart after all.

● **unhelpful beliefs:** that is, our opinion of ourselves is defined by more absolute views – usually developed in our formative years – that we consider to be facts. For example, 'I am a selfish person', 'I cannot get on with others', 'I'll never make a success of my life'.

Don't worry too much about which you believe to be your problem, or whether it is a mixture of the two. You will be able to get rid of your Inner Critic just as easily.

How might you get rid of these feelings of worthlessness?

One answer is to set very high goals for yourself. Surely, if you can gain workplace promotion, become the perfect partner, lose weight, look fantastic, become good at a new hobby or interest, then you will stop feeling this way about yourself? By relying on these impossible goals to make you feel better, you consistently fail and your self-esteem falls even lower. This 'setting of the bar too high' is called perfectionism and we look at how you can get over this problem in Chapter 3.

As well as setting the bar too high, we can also find the goalposts constantly move. Losing half a stone may seem a great goal until we achieve it: then it doesn't seem enough. Getting 70 per cent in an exam may have been beyond your wildest dreams when you predicted failure, but once the mark is awarded and you notice how many people got 80 per cent or 90 per cent, 70 per cent doesn't seem such an achievement after all.

Where you fear rejection, the best solution seems to be to predict your rejection in advance and then take steps to avoid it happening. You tell yourself, 'I won't get the promotion and it will be completely humiliating – best not to even go for it.' 'If I say anything at the committee meeting, others will see how little grasp I have of the facts. Perhaps it would be best to stay quiet?' 'I can tell that my partner is losing interest – he was looking at the TV guide while I was speaking to him. It's obviously over, so why not ditch him first?'

What drives these 'certainties'?

Fear of failure is a favourite topic for your Inner Critic. It spends a lot of time telling you not only that you probably will fail, but that it will also be untenable if you do. Its solution is that you are better off not trying in the first place.

Imagine learning to ski and being told that you are good enough to go into the next class. Your Inner Critic immediately steps in and questions this. Supposing that isn't true? Supposing you can't cope and fall, injure yourself, make an idiot of yourself? You begin to feel anxious about improving your skiing. Perhaps it would be better not to give it a go, as you may fail? Yes, that is the answer; don't even bother; stay with the beginner group where you can ski within your comfort zone. How do you feel now? Relaxed – the anxiety is gone. What a relief. But you are still no better at skiing, and now you never will be. No chance of increased self-esteem in this area – you will forever recount to friends how you found you were 'no good at skiing'.

So your Inner Critic not only feeds you negative information, it offers solutions that are tempting to you since they reduce your anxiety and it abets you in avoiding situations you perceive to be difficult. However, although your anxiety is reduced, so is your self-esteem, and your negative perceptions are reinforced.

What might discourage you from taking a risk?

Many people with low self-esteem suffer not only from vulnerability to the comments of others but the accompanying feelings of 'unbearability' that go with them. For example, someone says they are fed up with brunette hair and are going to dye it blonde; you (with brunette hair) automatically think this person doesn't like *your* hair. A friend says she is house-hunting and looking for something with olde worlde charm; if you live in a modern house, what you hear is, 'I don't like *your* house'.

Another way of describing this is 'personalization'. We take much of what others say far too personally rather than appreciating that it is a generalized opinion. Further, having determined in our minds that we have been personally criticized, we don't have the resilience to brush it off mentally or even resolve to do something about it. We simply feel wretched, criticized and unliked, when actually it was only our over-sensitivity to general comments that caused this heartache.

And if you don't risk a little, what happens?

When we don't risk a little, it tends to alienate us from others. We feel that if others want to see us, they will contact us, so we don't get in touch. We turn down the social invitations we do receive in case we feel like a fish out of water if we do accept.

Here are some common examples of how low self-esteem can affect how we think and behave. Do you recognize any in yourself?

- **It's everyone else** – we tend to blame other people for our misfortunes: 'I would not have done this if he had not said that'. We decide that we have been unfairly treated, without considering why. We absorb negative ideas, such as 'bad things always happen to me'. The more inadequate we feel, the more critical we become – it is as though finding fault with others helps us build ourselves up.
- **Pay attention to me** – sufferers from low self-esteem rely on feed-in from others to make themselves feel good. They may feel upset if this attention is not forthcoming. For example, someone at a party is berated by their partner for not paying them enough attention while spending a lot of time talking to others. This is low self-esteem talking.
- **People pleasing** – we become so anxious to be liked that we spend much of our time trying to please others, often at the expense of our own well-being, in the hope that their appreciation of our servitude will help us to feel better.

- **Coffee or tea?** – we are so uncertain of our ability to make a good decision that we dither, procrastinate and become totally indecisive. This can lead to poor decision-making skills, which in turn reinforce the person's low self-esteem.
- **Poor me** – this is a disempowerment mentality. We tell ourselves that we are the victims of circumstances that are outside our control, an attitude which prevents us from taking responsibility for what is happening, and allows other people to push us around. The saying, 'Other people treat us as well as we allow them to treat us' has some merit.
- **Trying too hard to impress** – when we feel inadequate compared to those around us, we may attempt to rectify this by overdoing things in the wrong way. We may name-drop, refer to recent personal success stories, affect unnatural mannerisms in the way we speak, for example. The idea is to impress others and make them think more of us. In reality, we do ourselves a disservice and impress no one.
- **Over-competitiveness** – our need to be right all the time stems from a desperate need to prove ourselves to those around us. Logically, it is extraordinary to believe that beating everyone else at everything would win us more acceptance and approval from others. Yet this is a form that low self-esteem can take for many people.

These are some, though not all, of the ways that, in our attempts to increase our self-esteem, we end up lowering it even further. Please don't feel an outcast if you recognize some of these traits in yourself. We have all been guilty of some of them at one time or another. That is human nature. It is the *extent* to which we behave in these ways that can blight our lives.

One or two of the above situations at least are possibilities for us when our self-esteem is low and we aren't prepared to try a new way: to take a risk.

Self-assessment ✓

Task: Testing your self-esteem levels

Even when you feel your self-esteem is very low, some of these negative feelings come from discounting your strengths and abilities rather than not having any.

Answer the questions below by rating how strongly you agree or disagree with the statements. At the bottom of the test, add up your scores.

Scores: 4 = totally agree, 3 = agree most of the time, 2 = agree sometimes, 1 = agree occasionally; 0 = never.

I consider myself to be a fairly worthwhile person.	
I can take criticism reasonably well.	
I don't take remarks people make too personally.	
I attempt to encourage myself rather than criticize myself for my weaknesses.	
When I make mistakes, I don't see myself as a total failure.	
I expect most people to like me.	
I am socially confident.	
I make some contribution to society, even if only a small one.	
It doesn't especially upset me if others disagree with my views.	
While being aware of my shortcomings I actually quite like myself.	
I feel that my life is fairly well on track.	
I can usually deal positively with setbacks.	
I attempt not to compare myself with others.	
I have a sense of humour and can laugh at myself.	
I generally consider that life is interesting and fun.	
Total score	

Results:

60 You *may* have a problem! Self-esteem that is too high can be as dysfunctional as self-esteem that is too low. Alternatively, wow, well done!

45–59 Your self-esteem is fine.

30–45 You certainly need a boost, but you recognize some of your good points, so making positive adjustments should not be too difficult for you.

15–30 You are suffering unnecessarily from negative thinking about yourself. We hope that will have changed by the time you have worked through this book.

0–15 You have a very serious self-esteem problem. This book may be enough to help you, but if not, you might benefit from professional assistance.

Now look at the test again. Were you rather hard on yourself? This is a common feature of low self-esteem. Consider your answers again, thinking of any instances when you have felt a little more positive than you initially thought

One of the goals of this book is to encourage you to realize that you are someone of great value just because you exist. While you will learn to make positive changes, these will be to *enhance* your self-worth, not to *create* it. Aim to feel happy with yourself in spite of your weaknesses, and you will like yourself just as much as someone who scored 60 on the test above; more importantly, others will like you a great deal more.

Self-assessment ✓

Task

How far do you consider that you might already be worthwhile? Begin to focus on your present assets, not your future goals. Write down a few positive values intrinsic to you. Start with just three or four.

1 _____

_____

2 _____

_____

3 _____

_____

4 _____

_____

If this seems hard, reread the passage above about self-acceptance, and keep going until you have three or four qualities written down. How do you feel now?

Retaining stability in your thinking

A phenomenon of life is that even when we feel good about ourselves it takes only a few seconds to lose all our gains and feel bad about ourselves again. We can be swinging along the road quite happily, feeling great, excited about the day ahead and then, guess what? We inadvertently catch sight of our reflection in a shop window. Suddenly, we see that our hair looks a mess, our nose is too long, the general impression is, well, not great. The spring goes out of our step and we start ruminating about our lack of attractiveness. Our confidence drains away, and the day doesn't seem so exciting and full of potential any more.

Does this sound familiar? Why do you think this happens? Your Inner Critic is at work again. The reason that the Inner Critic is so powerful is that it is working hard all the time. It rarely takes a break or goes on holiday. Because it works all day, every day, you become conditioned to believe this Inner Critic. It defines how you see yourself. Therefore, you believe that you will only feel good about yourself if you can silence it or block it out somehow. This is possible, up to a point. You may feel that you can prove it wrong by achieving something positive, for example, losing weight, winning a competition, receiving praise at work, wearing a designer outfit that you know looks good. But these feel-good factors only last for so long.

The feel-good factors are time-limited because these are things that are *external* to you. Your Inner Critic is not in charge of externals. It is in charge of the view you have of *yourself*. For example, someone complimenting you on a good piece of work is very uplifting. But once you find yourself struggling over the next project, your view might lean towards 'I got lucky with that last piece of work; now I am back to having difficulties that will show up my poor skills'.

Please ensure that you understand this very important point: our Inner Critic ensures that we are conditioned to think negatively about ourselves, which is why it is so hard to gain confidence and so easy to lose it again. We won't defeat our Inner Critic by constantly achieving external successes to countermand it, but by becoming so comfortable with ourselves that it is rendered useless and disappears.

Self-assessment ✓

Task: Testing your personal view of yourself

Here is a test that I give to many of my clients, half of which they find easy, and half of which they find very difficult. This will take a few minutes, so set aside some time to give it a go. First, take off your watch and set it beside you. You need to time yourself as you do this test, so don't start until you have made a note of the start time. For the first part of this test, start now.

List below your Top Ten weaknesses or faults:

1 _____
2 _____
3 _____
4 _____
5 _____
6 _____
7 _____
8 _____
9 _____
10 _____

Stop the clock! Note how long that took you. Time taken: ....
Now start the clock again, and complete the second part of this test.

List below your Top Ten qualities and strengths:

1 _____

2 _____

3 _____

4 _____

5 _____

6 _____

7 _____

8 _____

9 _____

10 _____

Stop the clock again. Note how long that took you. Time taken: ......

What have you discovered? We suspect that:

● you found the first part of the test much easier than the second part
● you may have wished for more space for the first part of the test, yet were scratching about to find 10 points for the second part
● your time record will show that you took a great deal longer to complete the second part of the test than the first.

What does this tell you? That you are a person with hundreds of faults and few good qualities? Or that your view of yourself is defined by a negative thinking style that you may actually be aware of but feel unable to do anything about?

The second view is almost certainly going to be the real problem, but do you know what? It doesn't matter whether you believe either the first or the second view. All that matters is that you are comfortable with yourself however you are. This is the core concept that you will learn as you work through this book. Once you begin to truly accept yourself, you will start to like yourself as well. Life is as good as your relationship with yourself.

The connection between thoughts and feelings

By now you have an idea of how negative thinking about yourself can cause low self-esteem. Now we would like you to take on board a further notion. Having negative thoughts isn't actually what upsets us. It is the *emotions* such thoughts engender that cause us pain and distress. If you think you are a 'born loser' but the feeling that this generates for you is calm acceptance (unlikely, but bear with me for the sake of example), you will feel OK. If the feeling that this thought generates is total despair, you will feel anything but OK.

Low self-esteem is problematic because it makes us feel badly about ourselves. Our thoughts generate these feelings.We *feel* the way we *think*.

At this point, you may wish to argue with this notion. You may still believe that the way you feel about yourself is due to external circumstances: other people failing to give you help and encouragement; poor parenting; lousy circumstances and bad breaks that have caused reverses in your life. However, this isn't quite true.

Case study

Meet Peter. As he walks down a corridor to his office, he passes Rob. 'Hi, Rob,' says Peter, giving him a friendly wave. Rob walks on by and fails to acknowledge Peter at all.

If you were Peter, would you feel:

- upset ('Rob obviously doesn't like me.')?
- angry ('How rude. He couldn't even be bothered to say hello.')?
- amused ('Silly idiot – he must have forgotten his glasses.')?
- concerned ('He was obviously very preoccupied. I wonder if everything is OK?')?
- equable ('Oh, well, Rob isn't always over-friendly.')?
- disappointed ('He didn't notice my new outfit.')?

To summarize, here we have:

- One event – two men passing in the corridor.
- Six different thoughts about the event.
- Six different feelings ….

Why did we not finish the last bullet point? Why did we not say 'Six different feelings about the event'? Because the feelings were *not* generated by the event. The feelings were generated by the *thoughts* about the event.

Reviewing behaviour

Task

Think through another example of alternative possibilities.

Jane is waiting in a restaurant for her friend, Liz. They have not seen each other for several months and Jane is very much looking forward to meeting up again. Then she gets a text from Liz to say she is held up at work and will be late. Jane waits on in vain – Liz doesn't turn up at all.

Write down how many different interpretations Jane could make of this event. See how many you can come up with. What emotion is Jane likely to feel as a result of each different interpretation of what has happened?

Does this idea now make sense to you? This is an exceedingly important point, the foundation upon which you will create good self-esteem. It means that instead of having to change all your life circumstances, you can work on changing your thinking – a much less daunting prospect – and this will change the way you feel.

This should help you begin to see the possibilities for change and that they are within your reach. In Chapter 4 we will reintroduce this concept as part of a way of improving your self-esteem called cognitive behavioural therapy.

Self-assessment ✓

Task: Your own self-esteem profile

Think about the lessons of your early life. For example, if you are shy with strangers, think about the opportunities you had (or didn't have) to talk to adults in such a way that you felt an equal rather than a child. If you find it hard to stand up to people, think about how those in authority reacted if you 'rebelled' in any way. Look at characteristics you consider personal weaknesses and see if you can find a point in your early life where these ideas might have begun. Write down your thoughts.

Writing these down may help you to understand how your low self-esteem gradually developed and will, hopefully, normalize it for you. Some aspects of our development naturally arise from the experiences of our formative years, but this does not mean that we need to carry them into adulthood without questioning their accuracy, as you are going to do now.

What I would like you to notice here is that the corrosive power of low self-esteem comes largely from external circumstances. This is natural. A concept that will help you overcome this is self-acceptance. When you adopt the idea of self-acceptance, you begin to value yourself *in spite of* what others think. Our low self-esteem may have developed owing to the negative views and comments (both perceived and real) of significant others in our lives. If we can develop enough resilience to value ourselves in spite of what others may think, we will begin to feel much better about ourselves.

Developing the idea of liking ourselves 'no matter what' will give us a much stronger base for self-esteem than being dependent on our achievements and external feed-in. This is self-acceptance in action.

Self-esteem is like a rickety old ladder; it can wobble a great deal. If our mood drops, so can our self-esteem, and vice versa. We can also feel especially confident in certain areas of our lives – super-confident even – and yet hopelessly inadequate in others. Some people say to me,

'I am completely confident in my workplace, but seem unable to sustain any sort of personal relationship and feel a total failure in this area.'

The role of beliefs in maintaining low self-esteem

In our daily lives, most of us experience many events that make us feel good about ourselves. We get good jobs, enter into loving relationships, create reasonably satisfying lives. So why does low self-esteem not go away for some of us? The answer, touched on briefly earlier in this chapter, is the beliefs that we have created about ourselves over many years. The mistake we make is that we then confuse beliefs with facts.

When our faulty, negative beliefs developed long ago they can morph, in our minds, into unchangeable facts and truths. Now you can hopefully begin to see that these are simply beliefs, and beliefs, by their very nature, can be changed and replaced with more optimistic, helpful beliefs.

Case study

Melissa was a bright student at school. However, her home life was poor, with an absent father and a mother who escaped her own inadequacies by drinking heavily. When drunk, she became abusive, and Melissa bore the brunt of this, for the simple reason that she looked very much like her absent father. When she tried to study at home, her mother told her that her father was stupid and therefore so was she, so what was the point of studying.

Melissa managed to keep her mother's beliefs at bay until she got low grades in one of her tests. For the first time, she began to wonder if what her mother told her was true. She then feared her next test as she realized that – in her own perception – perhaps she *was* rather stupid. Because of this anxiety, Melissa struggled with her next test and did poorly. Melissa now took this as proof that her mother was right. There was no point in trying, as it was a waste of time.

Sadly, Melissa consequently failed at school and achieved very little in her adult life. However, in Melissa's mind, this correctly reflected her low value and status in life, so it never occurred to her to do anything about it.

Melissa's story explains how low self-esteem is maintained. Melissa confused a **belief** with a **fact**. When Melissa failed her second test, instead of looking for rational reasons to explain why this might have happened, reasons she could have worked on (e.g. being over-anxious, misreading a question, not having studied hard enough), she accepted her 'stupidity' as the cause of her failure, and her failure as evidence of her stupidity.

Low self-esteem prevents you from accepting yourself as a valuable human being. You can achieve many positive accomplishments in your life and still suffer from low self-esteem. This is because there is a difference between an acceptance of your abilities on an intellectual level and an acceptance of yourself on a personal level.

Diary/journal write-in

Task

Take one negative belief about yourself, e.g. I'm hopeless at sport. Next, write down where this belief came from.

What evidence do you have to support it? Write down at least three different pieces of evidence here – one is not enough.

Now think about this for a while, and then write down any evidence you may have to challenge this view. This can be as simple as 'I've never even tried football, so it is only an assumption that I would be useless at it'.

Negative belief

_____

Evidence for this:

1 _____

_____

2 _____
_____

3 _____
_____

Evidence that challenges this:
_____
_____
_____

Don't worry if you find this difficult. You are just learning to stretch your thinking at this stage, and to appreciate the difference between beliefs and hard facts.

Chapter summary

In this introductory chapter we have looked at:

- how your faulty beliefs about yourself can become established
- how understanding this will support you in your movement towards change, as you can now appreciate that it is not who we are but our perceptions of who we are that cause us to doubt ourselves.

While you probably intrinsically know this, you need to remind yourself strongly that thoughts and beliefs are not facts and truths. Support yourself with this exciting premise, as it means we can change: we cannot change facts, but we can change what we think and what we do.

You have also learned that your negative, self-deprecating thoughts amount to an Inner Critic who will persistently tell you where you have gone wrong and what your weaknesses are. This book will show you that this is a fragile friend who, with the right skills and determination, can easily be defeated. We all have Inner Critics to a greater or lesser extent. It is only when this imaginary entity starts to spoil your life that you need to act to get rid of it. This is what you are doing now.

You will already have some ideas about what would help you, personally, to feel better, so Chapter 2 will help you to set goals for yourself. It is important to set your goals before you embark on using the skills and techniques you will learn to help you achieve them. Once you have turned vague statements such as 'I'd like to feel better about myself' into specific goals, such as, 'I'd like to be more at ease in social situations', 'I'd like to be more optimistic', 'I'd like to be in a meaningful relationship', then you will find it much easier to change and move forwards.

CHAPTER 2

Creating specifically defined goals

Overview

In Lewis Carroll's famous story *Alice's Adventures in Wonderland*, Alice underlines the importance of knowing where you want to go before you set off down any path. Now is the time to start setting your own personal goals for achieving good self-esteem and this chapter will show you how.

This may seem a boring start when you are itching to get on. However, it is how we start out with CBT, which is a very goal-oriented therapy. It spends time working out what the problem is, what maintains the problem and what the solution to the problem might be. To achieve this, CBT has to work with **goals**, and it is very important that you have set some goals for yourself before you start using CBT skills and techniques. Goals are your yardstick. They are a measure, on a chapter by chapter basis (and certainly between the start and the end of the book) of how you are progressing. Ensure you have your pad and pen (or other note-taking device) to hand for this chapter as you will be constructing and filling in a goal sheet that you will want to keep by you.

Goal-oriented or not?

Here are some questions to start with.

1   Am I someone who regularly sets goals for myself?
2   Do I tend to achieve the goals that I set?
3   What do I want to achieve from reading this book?

4   How do I think this book will help me to reach this goal?
5   Do I have a definite plan or simply a vague idea?

Answering these questions will give you a good general idea of whether or not you work in a goal-oriented way (questions 1 and 2) and if so, whether you are planning or setting goals for your CBT reading and learning (questions 3, 4 and 5). You may already be naturally good at setting goals. However, it is more likely that your goals are rather vague, e.g. 'to improve my self-esteem'. While a worthy goal, everyone will have different reasons for wanting to improve their self-esteem – and self-esteem isn't all-pervading. I work with people who are very confident in certain areas of their lives but totally lack this quality in others, e.g. some people are a whizz in the workplace but cannot handle personal relationships. I meet people who have terrific social lives on a superficial basis but flounder when faced with the intimacy of a deeper one-to-one relationship, and people who have no problems in this area but feel unappreciated in their job. So you do need to set specific, personal goals, to tackle both the extent of your low self-esteem and the areas in which you feel better self-esteem would make a real difference to you.

Consider setting yourself small goals for each chapter of this book. Some chapters will be more important to you than others, and for those that are, ask yourself what you would like to have learned by the chapter end. Or read the chapter through and if you cannot envisage clearly what you feel you have achieved, go through the chapter again until you gain what you want from it.

Goals and goal-setting

Before we move on to specific skills for overcoming low self-esteem, let's look at goals and goal-setting.

A goal refers to what you are totally committed to achieving. Think long and hard about what it is that you really wish to achieve – within a month, three months, six months or a year's time – and be honest with yourself about this.

As a general rule, it's inadvisable to set goals for beyond a year's time because your priorities may change; plus setting very long-term goals makes them seem an impossibly long way off. Keeping the time frame for goals short means they will appear as more than just a distant dream.

Mini-goals are the stepping stones which guide you to achieving your goals. They must be verifiable in some way, whether that's statistically – 'the more I do this the better I get at it' – or by some other achievable concept, such as actually getting the job or relationship that you want. It's crucial that your mini-goals lead you logically towards your overall goal and are quantifiable. The great thing is, after each mini-goal is achieved, you are rewarded with a warm feeling of satisfaction and increased confidence.

As with your goals, your mini-goals should be well thought-out. The time you take to draw up your goals and mini-goals will ultimately ensure that they are accurate, realistic and flexible – and that they are right for you.

When you've achieved your goal or goals (as a result of achieving all the mini-goals along the way), it will be time to set a new goal, and so the process starts again. However, this doesn't mean that you have to constantly set challenging goals. It could be a goal as simple as maintaining what you have achieved so far.

Using your understanding of where you are now to set new goals for yourself. 'What do I want to achieve?' or 'How do I want things to be different?' are good basic questions in goal-setting. Stephen Covey, the author of *The Seven Habits of Highly Effective People*, makes a brief but important statement when he says, 'Begin with the end in mind'.

Sometimes we describe our goals in a negative way – knowing what we don't want can be easier to describe than knowing what we do want. This isn't helpful, in the same way that setting unachievable goals that can only lead to failure and disappointment isn't helpful. So goal-setting is more than writing down a few ideas. It is a skill that is vital to setting you off on the right track.

Case study

Mary's daughter was getting married and her excitement was palpable. Mary wanted to be sure that this was the very best day of her daughter's life and to share this joy with her fully. Plans started to be made, dates were set, invitation lists drawn. Everything was moving forward nicely except for one thing: Mary's self-esteem was very low because of her weight. Always a large woman, the pounds seemed to be piling on now and Mary's attempts to stem the tide had little effect. Cutting out sugar and hoping that would do it hadn't made much difference. Mary felt ashamed of how she would look on her daughter's wedding day: how fat everyone would think her, what a glutton, what a pig, no self-discipline, etc. etc. So Mary decided on a drastic step – she would have a week of liquids only. This lasted until the evening of the first day, when a chocolate bar became too alluring to be ignored and everything went to pot. Then someone suggested exercise would make a difference – but what to do? Mary tried skipping, jogging (for about two minutes before she became breathless) and running up and down stairs, which was very dull and nearly caused a sprained ankle. A cabbage soup diet followed, then one that involved only eating protein, but these diets were so hard to follow that the results were negligible. Mary was making so much effort but nothing much was changing. Where was Mary going wrong? The answer was given by the slimming club she finally attended at a friend's suggestion. Up until then Mary had no *specific* goals, just wild hopes combined with a willingness to try, but not especially stick with, anything. After four weeks at the club (and with three weeks to the wedding day) Mary had shed eleven pounds! The reason for this success was simple. The slimming club made Mary define her goals exactly.

- How much weight did she want to lose overall?
- When did she want to lose it by?
- What did this mean her weekly goal would be?
- Was this realistically achievable or should it be adjusted?
- What choice of diet would she undertake?
- How would she shop for the food she would need?
- When would she do it?
- How would she handle cravings?

> For the first time, Mary had *written down* objectives and goals. She had lots of tiny, manageable and achievable steps to take that gave her optimism and success, and a target that got closer and closer and was achievable. As Mary learned, the more specific your goals are, the more likely you are to achieve them.

Researchers in the USA tracked a group of college students over the following 30 years. They discovered that those who had written down their goals (3 per cent) had succeeded in achieving them. A further 58 per cent had goals in their heads as they left college and they had far less success. The remainder of the students left college without any goals in mind, and most of any future good fortune was down more to good luck than any planning. So write your goals down and stick with them!

Success breeds success

In the the USA in the 1960s, the advertising industry took off and being a salesman was deemed a good way to make money. Most companies set the bar high for achieving bonuses from sales figures and if someone achieved the set target, this target was then raised for the next round of sales. In the end, this could be demoralizing and many salespeople gave up. At this time, the computer industry was also booming and IBM became the IT industry giant of the era, with excellent profits from selling computers in vast numbers. Investigating why IBM salesmen were so successful, researchers found that IBM set *easy* targets for their salespeople rather than hard-to-reach ones; thus, most of their salespeople achieved their targets. IBM had hired psychologists to define optimum motivational goals for their salespeople, and it was discovered that by making the targets achievable the salespeople became very confident and motivated (unlike their demotivated colleagues in rival companies) and went out and sold even more computers.

So the lesson is: make your targets achievable. You will feel a surge of success when you reach them and this will encourage you to continue. Learn from the IBM psychologists of the 1960s!

The characteristics of good goal-setting

Achievable goals have a set of characteristics that make them so:

- Flexibility: ensure that your goals are flexible. Think of your goal(s) as a piece of plasticine whose shape you can adjust as you gather more information and perhaps prefer a new direction. Don't set your goals in stone. Good goals have built-in flexibility and can be adjusted as you, your life and your personal desires change. What you are doing now is just a start.
- A variety of time frames; when you are setting goals, think about them in terms of short-, medium- and long-term goals. Set yourself short-term goals that you could reasonably achieve within, say, a week, or even a day; medium-term goals, which could be achieved within a month or two; and long-term goals which you might work on long afterwards, especially emphasizing positive changes and targets for personal growth.

The well-known SMART model for goal-setting, taught on business courses world-wide, is just as useful for you when setting your own goals. SMART stands for:

Specific
Measurable
Attainable
Realistic
Timely

Any goals you set should be able to meet each of the above criteria.

Specific

Goals should be straightforward and emphasize what you want to happen. Being specific helps us to focus our efforts and clearly define what we are going to do.

Specific is the what, why and how of the SMART model.

- **What** are you going to do?
- **Why** is this important to do at this time?
- **How** are you going to do it?

Ensure the goals you set are very specific, clear and easy. Instead of setting a goal to feel better about yourself or be more socially confident, set a specific goal that states exactly what would make you feel better about yourself or more confident, e.g. to be able to ask out the pretty girl who often smiles at you in the pub.

Measureable

If you can't measure it, you can't manage it; choose a goal with progress that is measurable, so you can see the change occur. How will you know when you reach your goal? Be specific! 'I want to be confident enough to join a bridge group that starts in November' is a specific target that can be measured. 'I want to be more socially confident' is not as measurable.

Attainable

When you identify goals that are most important to you, you begin to work out ways to achieve them. You develop the attitudes, abilities and skills to reach them. You may begin seeing previously overlooked opportunities to bring yourself closer to the achievement of your goals.

You probably won't commit to achieving goals if you set them too far out of your reach. Although you may start with the best of intentions, the knowledge that it's too much for you means your subconscious constantly reminds you of this and stops you from even giving it your best shot.

Realistic

In this context, 'realistic' means something that you are likely to be able to stick with in the long term. If you are shy, deciding never to turn down another social invitation again, for example, is highly unlikely to succeed. A more realistic goal might be to start accepting invitations to occasions with just a few close friends.

Timely

Achieving your goal(s) within a specific time frame is vital. Your commitment will be half-hearted if you know you can start and finish at any time as there is no sense of urgency to act. But do make your time frame realistic. All your goals must have at least some chance of success.

Working out your goals

While the SMART model is very useful for assessing the efficacy of your goals, first you need to think about what they will be.

Behaviour changing strategy

Task

Imagine for a moment that whatever you wished for could actually happen, as if with the wave of a magic wand. Note down what your hopes and dreams would be in these circumstances.

Perhaps you have written something like:

- I wish I could meet the right person for me.
- I wish I had more financial security.
- I wish I had the courage to change my job.
- I wish I was closer to my sister.

Now rewrite whatever you have put, replacing 'wish' with the phrase 'would like'.

Can you see or feel a difference in these statements? What do you consider this to be? While 'would like' has a positive ring to it, 'wishing' is actually negative. Unless you have some supernatural power, wishing has never changed anything. Stating that we would like something to be different is much more positive, and a better starting point for change.

Sometimes we make the mistake of stating our goals in a negative way, such as:

- I don't want to be lonely any more.
- I don't want to keep worrying about money.
- I don't want to work for this company all my life.
- I don't want to feel ill any more.

These types of goals are often referred to as 'dead man's goals', meaning that the goals could be achieved by someone who is dead, when clearly all worries would disappear. However, for the living, it is less about knowing what you don't want and more about knowing what you do want. So turn 'I don't want to work for this company all my life' into 'I want to have found a new job by the end of the year'. How much more positive a ring does that have to it?! It also requires a strategy to be planned to achieve this 'want' – a positive start to a likely positive change.

When you have identified areas that are causing you problems and that you would like to be different, you have your goals. Log them as a **goal list** of issues to work on.

Once you have a list of goals, your next step is to prioritize them. You are unlikely to be able to achieve everything at once and it is important not to jump back and forth from one thing to another. A good way to prioritize things is to give them each a value rating. Someone I knew had a new Porsche at the top of his list, and spending more time with his family at around fifth place. However, once he had given honest ratings to their value to him, he found that the car dropped down the list and being with his family more rose to the top.

Self-assessment ✓

Task

Prioritize your goals. Which is the most important to you and why.

Ask yourself: 'Which goal would I sacrifice the others for?' The answer can certainly adjust your original priorities.

Getting started

Most people assume that you should start with the highest priority on your list, but this is not always the case. Using your SMART model, look at the time element. Some goals need to be tackled urgently to avoid a crisis, e.g. 'If I can't feel more confident about my relationship, I may drive my partner away'. Other goals might make an immediate improvement to your life, e.g. 'The sooner I gain the confidence to talk to my boss about the ideas I have about the company, the sooner I will be considered a valued member of staff/gain a promotion'. If any of your goals fall into one of these categories, decide which is the most important and, ignoring other factors, place it at the top of your goal list.

Where time is not pressing, give your goals a further rating on a scale from 'hardest to achieve' to 'easiest to achieve'. These ratings will help you resolve the question of which to tackle first. It is helpful if you start with some easier goals and those where change is likely to occur rapidly, in order to give yourself hope and confidence. There is nothing wrong with doing things the other way round, though, and starting with to the hardest goal on the list. If you succeed there, then all else will seem easy. Bear in mind, however, the risk mentioned earlier in this chapter of setting yourself up for failure if you try to achieve too much too soon; ask yourself how you would be able to handle that compared to the more sure-fire successes of starting with the easier goals.

Now look through all your goals and, after considering the following questions, divide them into two sub-sections.

- Which of these goals can only be achieved by my doing something?
- Which of these goals might be achieved if I thought differently about them?

For example, if you find it difficult to get on with your boss at work, you have the choice of finding the courage to discuss this with him, or handing in your notice – or you could decide to work on not allowing him to continue to 'get' to you. You can decide from the various options what to set as your goal. However, if your low self-esteem is caused by, for instance, the fact that you are not very tall, then your goal will have to be the option of coming to terms with it!

Making decisions about your goals in this way will help you decide whether you want to work cognitively or behaviourally or both. This will then be built into your plan of action.

Reviewing behaviour

Task

Now is the time to put into practice what you have learned about goal-setting so far. (Don't worry at the moment about how you will achieve these goals – this book will teach you exactly how to do this as you work through it.) Start out by:

- setting out a list of 'wishes and wants'
- using what you have learned to turn these into positive possibilities
- using the SMART model to assess their viability as you set them out
- prioritizing them as suggested above
- dividing your list into action-oriented goals and thought-changing goals.

When you write your goals down, it's helpful to do so in the form of a chart. This will give you greater clarity than a simple list. You can develop your own chart, but below is an example that you might like to consider.

Main goal	Time frame	Mini-goals	Time frame	Action achieved/ revised
To work through this book and apply my learning to my personal situation(s)	6 months	To work on one chapter at a time and have confidence in my understanding before I move on	1 chapter a week	
To identify specific positive changes I wish to make to my life	immediately	To identify the small steps I can make towards achieving my main goal(s)	4 weeks	

Use your goal plan to work out your needs. List very specifically the actions you need to take in order to achieve them, e.g. 'To lose weight' is too vague – say how much weight, by when and exactly how do you plan to do it.

Remember that goals need to be flexible – that piece of plasticine that you can mould and change – because as you develop strategies for meeting them, you may find that you wish to change them.

Achieving your goals depends on your ability to take action.

Chapter summary

In this chapter you have learned that you need to set your goals before you move further towards the skills and techniques of overcoming low self-esteem. You will now be able to ensure that you set out your goals clearly and specifically; vague goals will achieve nothing as they are too hard to quantify.

As goal-setting can be time-consuming, do be prepared to spend time on it and don't rush through it. In therapy terms, it is easy to spend whole sessions simply working on goals and putting a structure in place for them.

Review your goals constantly. As mentioned earlier, our goals can change as our circumstances (or desires) change, and it is fine to restructure them at any point. They are cast in plasticine, not concrete. When you have achieved your goals, always set new ones, even if this is simply the maintenance of the goal(s) you have achieved so far. Don't allow yourself to lose the gains you have made.

We have already discussed how beliefs are not facts or truths but assumptions that we make, often quite early in our lives, and then never question. Chapter 3 will help you to understand how these beliefs can turn into a prison for our feelings about ourselves and, more importantly, how to escape from this.

Striving for perfection

Overview

To sufferers of low self-esteem, the idea of being regarded as perfect sounds like the answer to everything. Unfortunately, the opposite is the case. Perfectionism is actually a barrier to good self-esteem. So if you suffer from it, this chapter will:

- give you the support you need to be kinder to yourself and appreciate yourself without constantly feeling that you 'fall short'
- help you to set your goals from Chapter 2 more accurately and realistically.

What is perfectionism?

It is hard to define 'perfection' absolutely, so you are chasing constantly moving goalposts. We also tend to set 'being perfect' (at a particular thing or in general) as a goal and regard anything less than perfect as failure, thus reducing our self-esteem rather than enhancing it.

Many people's self-esteem is driven by unhelpful thinking about the standards they should be able to reach in order to feel good about themselves. Are you one of these people? Many of the clients I work with are. A common factor is that they are almost always extremely bright and intelligent, and are usually doing very well in life. Yet their self-esteem remains low because they are not achieving the perfect way of being that they believe they should attain.

Perfectionism = setting yourself up for failure. This is because it is almost impossible to get a perfect score. In many cases, it is impossible to know what that would be. For example, is there a cast-iron, concrete definition of 'perfect' beauty? Is there one for being a perfect pianist, or mathematician? What about a perfect parent? How would you even know if you had reached perfection? Even being the best in the world at something doesn't mean that you are perfect at it. So by trying to be perfect, you will almost certainly fail every time.

If you are a perfectionist, i.e. if you can recognize what we are discussing here as pertinent to you, then you may say that you do have your own definition of what is perfect when you undertake tasks or work on yourself in any way. However, this personal definition is likely to be both unrealistic and elusive. You may think you will know it when it arrives, but most perfectionists have difficulty in accepting perfection as being anything other than just out of their reach.

The saddest part about what is a serious condition is that it works on the law of diminishing returns. Attempting to be perfect can occupy a lot of time that could be more productively spent focusing on something else. You may recall teachers at school explaining the art of doing well in exams. It was always to divide up your time so that you could answer all the questions, and then spend only that specific amount of time on any one question before moving on to the next. Why was this? I am sure you understood it: the majority of the marks came from giving a reasonable answer. There were very few extra marks available for a perfect answer, and the loss of marks from not having enough time to answer all the other questions could even mean an exam failure. So teachers preached to us the advantages of four adequate answers rather than one perfect answer.

It will be hard for you to acknowledge that either 'being OK' or 'doing OK' is good enough if perfectionism dogs you, but this chapter will help you to overcome this difficulty.

The link between perfectionism and self-esteem

How is perfectionism likely to affect your self-esteem? The answer, for most people, is 'hugely'. It means that, no matter how well you do, you are never able to see yourself as the success you would like to be. It also means that you may spend so much time – over and above what others would consider normal – on individual tasks and targets that you then fall behind in other areas. This also weakens your ability to see yourself as anything other than someone who is failing all round.

Research shows that perfectionism usually develops in our formative years: being in the football team wasn't good enough unless you were captain; playing an instrument wasn't enough – you needed to be the best at it. As commented on earlier, doing well in an exam can mean little when others do even better. The legacy for many young people is the feeling that no matter what they do, it is never good enough. For some youngsters, feeling the least loved of siblings can cause perfectionist tendencies as they strive to show their parents that they can do things perfectly. Failure to form desired friendships, rejection generally, and particularly in hoped-for romantic relationships, can also lead to a strong sense of not being up to scratch.

You may carry this feeling with you into adulthood as a self-defeating belief, and you will constantly criticize yourself and feel worthless because you aren't achieving a standard that you personally consider to be perfect. You can change, however. Change is not too hard – and it is important. You can teach yourself to see things differently – not seeing yourself as a failure but someone who is quite normal, with normal strengths and weaknesses – and feel more confident.

Reviewing behaviour

Task: Shifting perfectionist thinking

Write down three beliefs you have about striving for perfection. For example:

- I must always try to be perfect.
- Anything less than complete success is failure.
- Others will think less of me if I make mistakes.
- I cannot live with myself if I let my standards slip.

Using the headings below, take each attitude in turn and write down first what you see as the advantages to you of holding this view. Then write down any disadvantages to you of holding this view.

If you have any views where the disadvantages outweigh the advantages, can you come up with an alternative view that might be more helpful? If you can, write it down. If you cannot do this at the moment, don't worry. You will find this easier by the end of this section.

Perfectionist view 1

Advantages to you of holding this view:

_____

_____

_____

Disadvantages to you of holding this view:

_____

_____

_____

Can you find a more helpful view?

_____

_____

_____

Perfectionist view 2

Advantages to you of holding this view:

_____

_____

_____

Disadvantages to you of holding this view:

_____

_____

_____

Can you find a more helpful view?

_____

_____

_____

Perfectionist view 3

Advantages to you of holding this view:

_____

_____

_____

Disadvantages to you of holding this view:

_____

_____

_____

Can you find a more helpful view?

_____

_____

_____

The perfectionist perspective of others

Earlier in this chapter we asked you to consider why friends or
colleagues might not share your need to achieve such high standards
all the time. What answers did you come up with? For each of these
explanations, answer another question: Why does this matter? For
example, if you have put 'My colleagues are content with a lower
standard of work', ask yourself why that matters.

Reviewing behaviour

Task

Now try a similar exercise to the last task but for friends and/or colleagues' achievements if they seem content with less perfection than you.

Ask yourself the advantages and disadvantages to *them* of their approach. (This isn't about how *you* see it, but how you think that they might see it.) For each person, make a subjective assessment of their self-esteem (1 = low, 10 = high).

View of friend/colleague 1

Advantages to them of holding this view:

_____

_____

_____

Disadvantages to them of holding this view:

_____

_____

_____

Subjective self-esteem rating for friend/colleague (1–10) = ...

View of friend/colleague 2

Advantages to them of holding this view:

_____

_____

_____

Disadvantages to them of holding this view:

_____

_____

_____

Subjective self-esteem rating for friend/colleague (1–10) = ...

View of friend/colleague 3

Advantages to them of holding this view:

_____

_____

_____

Disadvantages to them of holding this view:

_____

_____

_____

Subjective self-esteem rating for friend/colleague (1–10) = ...

The big question is: what does this tell you?
Write down what you have discovered and what it might mean.

Challenging perfectionist beliefs

Look again at the perfectionist beliefs you listed earlier in this chapter. These are **thinking errors**. What thinking errors are you making? We suspect that 'all or nothing thinking' (i.e. when we think that if something is not perfect, then it is hopeless) would be one of them. Become aware of other thinking errors, which we will look at in more detail in Chapter 5.

Before you can overcome perfectionist tendencies, it may be helpful for you to understand how you got them in the first place. While it is possible that your parents were always stretching you to achieve more, there can be other reasons as well, such as:

- parents constantly urging you to do better
- desperately needing to please a parent; this might be out of fear or love, e.g. if financial sacrifices have been made in order to ensure you received a good education
- sibling rivalry
- scholastic rivalry, perhaps through getting into competition with one or two other pupils to 'always be the best'

- feelings of inferiority, either at home or in adult personal relationships that taught you conditional love ('Unless I am perfect, my family/partner will not care for me')
- being abandoned, leading to either an 'I'll show them!' attitude or to you throwing yourself into something that won't harm or distress you as a panacea, such as work or academia.

Ideas about being perfect come from past experiences that, if we stop and think about them, are often no longer valid. We therefore don't need to keep following these old rules.

Self-assessment

Task

Write down where you feel your own perfectionist tendencies have come from. Based on the reason that you have worked out, write a sentence or two describing why you feel that you need to keep this perfectionism going.

Then ask yourself:

- do you really need to?
- are the reasons still valid, or are you carrying with you past beliefs that could be more helpfully replaced?

Behaviour changing strategy

Task

Taking the perfectionist thoughts that you used in the previous exercises, start to make a mental note of how you might positively and helpfully adjust these in such a way as to keep your self-esteem in good shape.

In the same way that you weighed up the advantages and disadvantages of your perfectionist beliefs earlier in this chapter (a type of 'cost-benefit' analysis), we would like you to do something similar using what you have discovered about the origins of your perfectionism.

Reviewing behaviour

Task

First, write down your perfectionist beliefs. Then consider:

- what are the advantages of continuing to be driven by this?
- what are the disadvantages of continuing to be driven by this.

Perfectionist belief 1

Advantages of continuing to be driven by this:

_____

_____

_____

Disadvantages of continuing to be driven by this:

_____

_____

_____

Perfectionist belief 2

Advantages of continuing to be driven by this:

_____

_____

_____

Disadvantages of continuing to be driven by this:

_____

_____

_____

Perfectionist belief 3

Advantages of continuing to be driven by this:

_____

_____

_____

Disadvantages of continuing to be driven by this:

_____

_____

_____

Bear in mind that we are not asking you to list the advantages to you of being successful. We are asking you to consider the advantages of basing your self-esteem on your success. Is it realistic to continue to think this way? What is the purpose now of continuing to prove something, either to yourself or to others? In other words, don't robotically continue to think 'I must do things perfectly'. Begin to examine what useful purpose this serves.

Ask yourself two more things:

- if a friend told you that they felt miserable and inadequate unless they achieved perfection in all that they did, what would you say to them?
- if you had a friend who seemed to succeed at everything they tried, but came across as rather driven and self-absorbed, how would you rate them for likeability?

Developing healthier values

If you could feel good without always striving for perfection, wouldn't this be much more relaxing? Develop a healthier value system by facing the origins of your perfectionism and asking yourself how much you need to keep striving in this way now. Think more in terms of likeability than 'right-ability' as you undertake tasks. Check how you feel as you perform tasks, thinking in this new way. Do you actually feel more relaxed and at ease with yourself?

Testing it out

Perfectionist thinking dictates that satisfaction from doing something is based on how effectively you perform. This isn't true, and testing it out will help you make changes to your life that will be very meaningful. Use a chart with the following headings to measure this subjectively.

- What I have to do
- Satisfaction rating I hope for from my performance (1–100%)
- Actual satisfaction rating (1–100%) and comments on the rating

- Rating for how effectively I consider I performed the task (1–100%) and comments on the rating
- How I feel now.

There is an example below for guidance.

Fill in your chart gradually but regularly, as you learn that the greatest pleasure and feelings of satisfaction come from the taking part and not the winning.

What I have to do	Satis-faction rating I hope for (%)	Actual satisfaction rating (%) and comments	Rating for how effectively I consider I performed (%) and comments	How I feel now
Mend garden fence	20%	90% Can't believe I actually did it!	30% DIY is not my thing, so it's not the best-done job in the world.	Pretty chuffed!
Give monthly presentation at work	90%	40% I do this every month, so of course I do it well. I expect it.	90% I obviously turn in the best performance I can and am good at my work.	Pleased it went well, but nothing more.
Game of tennis	60%	90% Got in a couple of good backhands, and had lots of fun.	40% I played poorly, even for my mediocre standard	Relaxed and happy. It's only a game, I've had great exercise and a drink with my friends afterwards.

Letting go of impossible goals and targets is a vital part of increasing self-esteem. How can you ever feel good about yourself if you constantly set such high standards that you will never achieve them and always feel that you have failed?

Chapter summary

In this chapter you have learned:

- to recognize any perfectionist tendencies within yourself
- to consider why people with good self-esteem don't need to be perfectionists
- how to enjoy doing something and achieve satisfaction from it without doing it 'perfectly'.

Having good self-esteem can erroneously be interpreted as being good or the best at something, and not achieving perfection can encourage us to call ourselves failures. But what is perfection? Is there any such thing or is it just a personal viewpoint, different for everybody? If so, attempting to achieve this elusive concept as a way of improving your self-esteem is almost always going to end in failure.

If you understand why others whose self-esteem is good don't need to be perfectionists, you will be on the way to achieving it for yourself. You can also discover that enjoyment and a sense of achievement can come from tackling things you may not feel you are much good at. A sense of achievement is vital to good self-esteem, and more important than meeting your expectations of doing something well.

Hopefully you are gaining a good idea of how low self-esteem can develop and, more importantly, what maintains it. You will understand why it is so hard to break free from negative thoughts but, with your new understanding there is new hope. How we feel about ourselves is simply a perception, not a reality (consider how many crooks think they are above the law, for example), and perceptions can be changed!

Now we move on to Part 2, where we are going to start actively tackling low self-esteem and converting you into someone who feels really good about themselves.

Tackle

Get to grips with what you need to do to make a change

CHAPTER 4

Introducing cognitive behavioural therapy

Overview

Feeling confident isn't something 'out there'. It is 'right here', within you, because happiness, confidence and feeling good about yourself are emotions, not life events, not something you can touch, feel, purchase or pursue.

Happiness is simply an emotion that we feel, dependent not on external events but on our thoughts about those events. Things often go wrong in our lives; people act selfishly towards us, we make mistakes, disappointments occur. If our thoughts about such events are negative – perhaps we blame other people, the weather, ourselves, for things going wrong – then these views will decide how we feel emotionally (angry, frustrated, anxious, resentful, for example) and possibly also how we behave as a result. In this chapter you will learn about an excellent tool, cognitive behavioural therapy (CBT), which will enable you to create and work on a plan for real change in your life.

The basic CBT model

Some readers may already have a grasp of the basic principles of CBT, but those who do not will benefit from reading this chapter so that you can understand the premise of CBT in its simplest form before we go further.

A 'cognition' is another word for a thought. Beck et al. (1979) describe it as, 'Either a thought or a visual image that you may not be very aware of unless you focus your attention on it.' You will understand this better by thinking about it yourself, rather than reading a explanation, so try the exercise below.

Reviewing behaviour

Task: Understanding the basic premise of CBT

Think of the most recent occasion when something went wrong and your thoughts were fairly negative. Perhaps something bad happened, or you felt that you acted in a way that disappointed you and that you regret?
Write down the following.

- What happened?
- What thought(s) went through your mind?
- How did you feel, both emotionally and physically? (Feelings can usually be described in a one word, e.g. happy, sad, cheerful, miserable etc., but we may feel several emotions at once). You may also have noticed feeling drained or tense, your stomach churning etc. Note down any physical feelings too.
- What did you do? Did you act in a way that made the situation better or worse?

Now think of a recent *good* event, or an occasion when you feel that you acted in a way that made you feel good about yourself and your thoughts were more positive. Answer the same question.

- What happened?
- What thought(s) went through your mind?
- How did you feel, both emotionally and physically?
- What did you do?

What connections can you make here? Write down any that occur to you.

How thoughts, feelings and behaviours are linked

Can you see a connection between what you thought about the event, how you felt and what you did? You will certainly have noticed that if you had negative thoughts, your emotions would also have been negative, you may have noticed adverse bodily sensations, and you may have reacted behaviourally in a less than positive way. On the other hand, where your thoughts were positive, it would be extraordinary if your emotions were not also upbeat, you would have felt physically energized, and acted very positively.

In other words, how you felt about the event depended on your view of the event rather than the event itself. This, in its simplest form, is the basic CBT model.

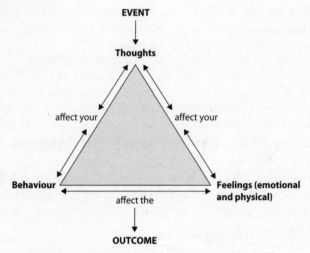

Our thoughts are not the only predictors of outcomes – thoughts on their own acutally have little effect on us – but they do play a very powerful role in shaping how we feel. You can think whatever you like, it is only the *emotions* that thoughts engender that delight or disturb us. It is the thought–emotion combination that is all-powerful, shaping our responses and reactions, which may in turn decide outcomes.

This is the basic premise of CBT, a therapy model that, if you learn how to apply it, will enable you to recognize some of your own styles and patterns of thinking, including those that create unhappiness and distress. You can learn how to counteract these so that you can deal with potentially upsetting situations in a more helpful way.

The great thing about CBT is that, once you understand the principles, you will not only be able to apply them to your own life, but also to helping others (and they might not even know you're doing it). You will learn to be your own life coach – it will enable you to get more out of the life you already have.

Our different levels of thinking

To learn how to feel good about yourself, you need to learn a little about the way your mind operates. When you are feeling down and have doubts, people often tell you to 'think positively' and 'look on the bright side'. Imagine if it were as easy as this?! Do you sometimes feel like responding, 'I would if I could?' Or do you sometimes agree, and actually try to do as you have been advised?

On the basis of this advice, we can simply say to ourselves, over and over, 'I am *not* selfish' or 'I *am* very attractive', and our self-esteem should increase in relation to how often we repeat these mantras.

The reason this does not work, however, is because our thoughts won't hold water if they are in direct contradiction to our basic beliefs about ourselves. These beliefs are not necessarily true (although they might be) but we *think* they are, and this is where the problem lies. You could have film-star good looks, but if you believe you have a big nose that makes you look ugly, then it doesn't matter how many times you look in the mirror and repeat to yourself that you are good-looking, you will never believe it.

You need to begin to check whether your beliefs are factually true or just **beliefs**. Do you really have a big nose, or is that what you see when you look in the mirror because someone at school once rudely suggested that you had? Does your nose *really* make you look ugly, or is that an **assumption** you have made: 'If I have a big nose, I must be ugly'?

Sometimes, our beliefs are right, in which case we can problem-solve to make changes. But challenging our beliefs – 'playing detective' to check their validity – is always the first place to start.

Reviewing behaviour

Task

Do you ever attempt to 'think positively' when your mind is flooded with self-defeating negativity? Does it work for you?

Consider when it makes a difference and when it doesn't.

Negative thoughts, negative assumptions and negative beliefs have already been mentioned. What is the difference between them? In defeating low self-esteem, it is important that you understand the relationship between them as well as their differences.

Imagine your thought processes are like a three-tier cake, looking a bit like this:

Day-to-day thoughts
('What an idiot I was to do that.')

Assumptions
('If this …. then that…')

Basic beliefs
('Truths')

Negative thoughts are the 'top layer' of our thinking. They automatically pop in and out of our minds: 'Oh, I've messed up there', 'I think I've just said the wrong thing', 'I can tell he doesn't like me', 'I'll never get this right' – your Inner Critic in full throttle! For this reason, we tend to call them **automatic negative thoughts**, and the moment something happens, there they are. No reasoning, no pondering or internal debating: just the first thought that comes into our head.

Characteristics of automatic negative thoughts are:

- they spring to mind without any effort
- they are event-specific, i.e. something happens to cause us to think this way

- they are easy to believe
- they can be difficult to stop
- they are unhelpful
- they keep your self-esteem low and make it difficult to change
- they are often *not true*.

These automatic negative thoughts may be difficult to spot to start with, as you are probably not aware that you have them, or you may define them as 'rational' thinking and see nothing negative about them. So the first step is to learn to recognize them. Just becoming aware of these thoughts can help you begin to think in a more helpful, constructive way.

Self-assessment ✓

Task

Write down what you consider to be negative characteristics about yourself. Do you consider these to be rational thoughts?

How many of the characteristics of negative thoughts listed above do these thoughts have? Tick these off and see how many ticks each thought has got.

What might this mean about your thinking?

Linking negative thoughts to negative beliefs

Negative beliefs are the 'bottom layer' of our thinking. We regard them as absolute; in our minds, they are not open to debate as we (often erroneously) believe them to be facts. We have negative beliefs about:

- ourselves ('I am worthless')
- others ('People always let you down')
- the world ('Crime is everywhere')
- the future ('Nothing will ever change').

Negative beliefs can be so deep that we rarely consider them or evaluate them: we just accept their existence and build our other thought processes around them. We see them as absolute truths, 'just the way things are', but they are very often wrong. Usually stemming from childhood, when we rarely, if ever, question what we learn, these beliefs can keep us trapped in our low self-esteem.

Case study

Anna's parents loved her dearly, but they decided that telling her that whatever she achieved, she could do even better would have a positive effect. However well Anna did, instead of being praised, she was told to 'try even harder next time'. If she got 80 per cent in a test, that was a failure and she must get 90 per cent next time. If she got 90 per cent, then only 100 per cent was good enough. While Anna's parents felt that they were encouraging her to stretch herself and achieve more, Anna, unsurprisingly, developed a negative belief about herself along the lines of 'no matter how hard I try, I'm just not good enough'.

Anna did get herself a good job. However, she was never able to fulfil her potential, as every time she started on a piece of challenging work, her belief that 'I'm just not good enough' would kick in and she would think, 'I won't be able to do as good a job as they want. I'll get it wrong and everyone will see how incompetent I am. I'll let someone else take it on, and stick to simple tasks I can't mess up.'

Telling Anna to think more positively and that she will do a good job won't help her at all, because it flies in the face of her basic belief that she isn't good enough. Similarly, you need to learn to identify unhelpful beliefs that prevent you from thinking more positively about yourself and your abilities, and to learn how to replace them with more realistic beliefs that will stop holding you back.

We are less aware of our negative beliefs than we are of our negative day-to-day thinking. This is because we convince ourselves that our beliefs are 'truths' and thus, don't need particular consideration or evaluation. Constantly remind yourself that negative beliefs are no more than a *point of view* that may not be true.

Self-assessment ✓

Task

Consider any negative beliefs you might have about yourself. Write them down. Use the criteria given earlier in this chapter to ensure that they are basic beliefs.

Ask yourself how strongly you believe each of them at this moment, using a scale from 1 = not much to 10 = absolutely.

When you finish this book, rerate the beliefs and see how much the strength of your beliefs has diminished.

Negative assumptions – the 'middle layer' of our thinking

Negative assumptions link our beliefs to our day-to-day thinking. In this sense, they are the 'middle layer' of our thinking. They also become our Rules for Living. For example, if you hold a negative belief that you are a boring person, you may make the assumption, 'If I talk to people socially, they will find me dull and uninteresting'. So when you receive a party invitation, you may think, 'I won't go. No one will want to talk to me.' Or you may go but decide, 'I'll just stand by myself in the corner and hope no one notices me. That way, I won't have to talk to people.' So you may develop a Rule for Living not to socialize, as you consider this will prevent your 'I am boring' belief being put to the test.

Anna, with her 'I'm not good enough' belief, might hold an assumption, 'If I stay on the bottom rung of the career ladder, doing simple work I can easily handle, then I won't lose my job.' Anna is developing a Rule for Living that it is better not to do anything that she finds difficult in order that her incompetence will never be discovered.

Self-assessment ✓

Task

Can you identify any Rules for Living of your own? Look back at any basic negative beliefs about yourself that you identified. Ask yourself how you cope with those beliefs on a day-to-day basis. For instance, if you believe you are unlikable, your Rule for Living is perhaps to be as nice as pie to everyone at all times to mitigate against this.

Write down three Rules for Living that you tend to use to overcome some of your self-defeating beliefs.

1

2

3

Identifying your Rules for Living

The good news is that as you gain in self-esteem and self-acceptance you will be able to consign these Rules to the waste bin. Remember, these thoughts, assumptions and beliefs are just a point of view, not facts. They are usually erroneous, and it is not too hard to replace them with more helpful, accurate and positive alternatives.

The table below gives an example of how an event can trigger an emotion that then generates self-critical thoughts. Now fill in examples of your own.

Emotion you felt	Event triggering the emotion	What you thought when this happened (*i.e. self-critical thoughts generated by your Inner Critic*)
Example: Anxiety	Client forgot important meeting	He isn't taking this seriously. He probably feels I'm not good enough to do the work.
1		

2		
3		

Self-defeating behaviour

If someone with low self-esteem gets turned down for a job that they wanted very badly, their Inner Critic may say to them, 'You're useless. You will never get a good job. There will always be other candidates far better than you.' In this negative thinking state, what is this person's most likely *behavioural* response? The likelihood is that their *behaviour* will mirror their *thinking*.

- They may stop applying for jobs altogether.
- They may set their sights lower and apply for jobs well below their capabilities.
- They may still continue to go for interviews but expect to do badly at them, which will be reflected in the impression they make, or fail to make.

This means that they are likely to remain unemployed, confirming that their negative thoughts and beliefs were correct. This will make the person feel emotionally low, and their self-esteem will sink even lower.

Self-assessment ✓

Task

Look back at the chart you filled in earlier, listing your negative thoughts and feelings.

Add a fourth column, with the heading 'Self-defeating behaviour', and write under that what you did as a result of your negative thoughts and feelings.

Bringing it all together

Let's bring all these thoughts, feelings and behaviours together, so that we understand what maintains someone's low self-esteem. Look at the diagram below, which offers an explanation of the possible effects of the negative thinking that can accompany low self-esteem.

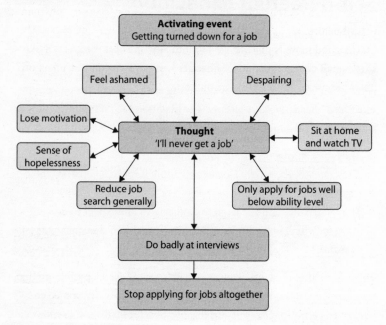

As you can see from the diagram (described in CBT terms as a **conceptualization** or **formulation**), thoughts, feelings and behaviour are all linked. This linking is what maintains the problem and keeps our self-esteem low.

Look closely at the arrows. They point in two directions, both outwards and inwards. Each negative emotion and action that you have in response to your negative thinking feeds back to you to reinforce your conviction that your negative views were correct. In other words, the emotions and actions driven by the thinking maintain the thinking.

Look again at this formulation. There is nothing here that is going to break this cycle of despair and hopelessness. It is feeding on itself so nothing changes. Yet the sad fact is that the negative thoughts that are causing this may be untrue.

The more we think negatively, the worse we feel, and the more negative our behaviour becomes. In turn, our negative behaviour causes us to feel even worse, and think even more pessimistically than we did before.

The good news is that we can tap into any one of these areas, make a few small changes, and those changes will have a knock-on effect on the other areas. The diagram below shows this.

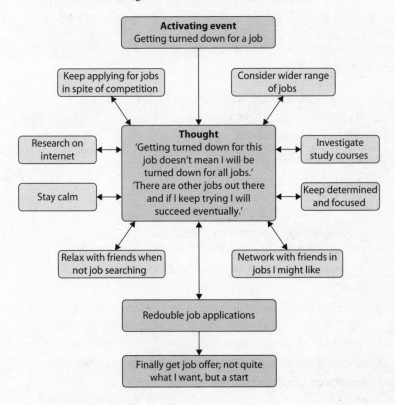

Can you see what is happening here? Look at the two formulations. The event was the same. Yet the event created thoughts which generated emotional responses and actions that either maintained and consolidated the problem or drove a way forward out of the problem. If you understand the importance of this, you will be well on the way to improving your own self-esteem.

Reviewing behaviour

Task

With the examples above as a guide, attempt to create a formulation of your own that may help to explain the maintenance of a particular problem that you have.

Using the most recent example of an event that caused you some upset, write down:

- what your thoughts were
- how you felt and acted as a result of these thoughts.

Look at what you have written. Did these thoughts, feelings and actions resolve your problem, or did they maintain it?

Chapter summary

This chapter has:

- introduced you to the principles of CBT
- given you a clear understanding of how the way we perceive a situation, rather than the situation itself, decides how we feel about it
- shown how what we think would alone have little effect on us; it is the effect our thoughts have on our feelings that have the great impact on our well-being
- explained about the different layers of thinking: thoughts, assumptions and beliefs.

Our thoughts not only decide how we feel, both physically and emotionally, they also usually decide what action we take, i.e. what our behaviour is. When our thinking and emotions are negative, the chances are that our behaviours will be also. If we believe we'll never get a job, aren't good enough to join the sports club, don't cope well at parties, then it is likely that negative behaviours will reflect these thoughts, in this case by not testing out the assumptions.

CHAPTER 5

Moving towards a healthier self-esteem

Overview

Appreciating the basic relationship between thoughts, feelings, actions and outcomes is an essential first step, as it helps us to identify where we may be going wrong. Now we will move on to look at how you can make the changes that will defeat your low self-esteem and replace it with a strong and healthily balanced view of yourself.

Once you get used to using these skills and techniques and feel more confident with them, they will help you to see that you can adjust your self-esteem levels in any areas of your life simply by practising a new way of looking at things. Some clients whose aim is to gain increased self-confidence tell me of all the things they feel unable to do because of low self-esteem. They say, 'When I have more confidence I will be able to do *this or that* …'. They learn that it is doing '*this or that*', perhaps many times over, that will give them the confidence they seek.

Replacing self-defeating thoughts and beliefs

You have learned how to identify your self-defeating thoughts, and the emotions and behaviour patterns that go with them. However, so far your Inner Critic has had the upper hand; now is the time to show your Inner Critic the door. Remind yourself strongly that how you feel is based on what you think. If you want to feel good about yourself, you need to think realistically, not negatively.

The best way to challenging your Inner Critic is by writing down your negative thoughts and emotions and then writing down more positive or realistic alternatives. This is called a **Thought Record** because although you are recording what has happened, the main focus is on what you *thought* about what happened. The more you practise filling in a Thought Record, the easier it becomes to spot these thoughts, and to understand the effect they have on how you feel.

First, write it down. Writing things down can be a chore: 'It takes so much time', 'I can never find a pen', 'Can't I just do this in my head?' NO! (Sorry.) Writing things down is far more powerful than just trying to think things through. It causes you to think really hard, and all the time you are writing, you are thinking. Remember our exam analogy earlier when we discussed perfectionism? How were we taught to study for exams? By having teachers talk to us relentlessly and hoping we would retain, in our heads, everything they said? Of course not. Teachers made us take notes, i.e. write things down, as they knew we would both understand and remember the written word much better than the verbal.

Take a look at the Thought Record below. You will see that it is an extension of the record you have already filled in. You might wish to copy out your Thought Record or take a photocopy. (This format will change again later in the book, so only make one or two copies to use until then.)

Filling in your Thought Record

Practise filling in the Thought Record, working across the table. Fill in each column for at least one negative thought. Don't worry if it does not come very easily at first. This is just a start, and here are some tips and ideas to turn this into a really useful tool for you.

- Rating your thoughts and emotions: you will see that you are asked to rate (subjectively) how strongly you believe your negative thoughts, the intensity of your emotion, and the strength of your belief in the alternative responses. This is so that you can check

A basic Thought Record

Date, time and what happened	What you thought when this happened *(How strongly do you believe this, on a scale of 1–10?)*	How you felt *(How strongly did you feel this, on a scale of 1–10?)*	Alternative thoughts *(Generate at least 2–3 alternatives; rate your belief in them, on a scale of 1–10.)*	How do you feel now? *(Rate any change now you have looked at things more positively)*

that you have picked the thought that generates the emotion. For example, if your negative thought is 'I am over-dressed for this function' and your emotion is 80 per cent panic, you may not have logged the right thought. Ask yourself *why* being over-dressed is causing you such anxiety and you will get closer to your real concern. The answer might be 'I will look completely out of place and everyone will laugh at me'. *Now* you have identified the thought which might cause such panic. This is an important point, as your Thought Record will not help you unless you are working with what really bothers you. So do take some time to consider what is *really* upsetting you.

- Finding alternative responses: you may initially find it hard to come up with alternative responses. This is because your natural tendency is to be self-critical, and to believe these self-critical thoughts to be true. Be very firm with your rebuttals. Really talk back to your Inner Critic. Try to come up with at least two or three alternatives, not just one. There are always several different ways of looking at the same thing. Find them.

- Lack of belief in the alternative: you may initially find that although you have come up with alternative thoughts, you don't really believe them. You still believe your self-critical thoughts more strongly. This will gradually change, and you will learn further skills to help you to reinforce your beliefs in a more positive outlook.

- Rating the strength of your emotions at the end of the Thought Record checks whether challenging the negative thoughts does in fact help you to feel better.

Once you are familiar with identifying negative thoughts, you can examine how unrealistic or unhelpful they are and whether they are useful to you. Studies have shown that doing this can improve your mood and make you feel more in control of your situation and your life.

Behaviour changing strategy

Task

Begin using your Thought Record on a daily basis. Set yourself a goal of challenging one negative thought each day for the next two weeks.

(As you get more used to doing this, you may eventually no longer need to write down your thoughts, but please ensure you do so initially.)

Using a Thought Record will help you to understand that to improve your self-esteem, it is vital to challenge your existing ways of thinking and acting, and to learn to replace them with alternative ideas about yourself that will raise your spirits and make you feel more confident and accepting. We want to help you develop a variety of skills and techniques in order to do this. A basic Thought Record is a start, but only a start. So let's look at other techniques for getting rid of your Inner Critic.

Recognizing distorted thinking patterns

We cannot emphasize enough that the feelings generated by low self-esteem – worthlessness, depression, anxiety, to name but a few – are caused by *distorted* thinking. Once you learn to challenge these thoughts, you will immediately change how you feel both about yourself and life in general.

Recognizing distorted thinking is not always easy. We assume that all our thinking is rational and 'correct'. In a good frame of mind it may be (though not always). But when we are in a poor frame of mind, our thinking can become negative and distorted without our realizing that this is happening.

The problem is that once we start making thinking errors we tend to stick with them. They become, as we have learned already, assumptions and beliefs that we retain unless we make an effort to recognize them and change them.

Psychologists have identified a number of common thinking errors that most of us make some of the time – and some of us make all of the time. If you know what these are, and recognize them, it will make your challenging rebuttals much easier to formulate.

Generalizing the specific

You come to a *general* conclusion based on a *single* incident or piece of evidence. For example, if you have a minor car accident, you decide you are a dangerous driver (and must never drive again). One failed recipe means you cannot cook, and wobbly stitching means you cannot sew. Someone treats you unfairly and you say, 'Nobody likes me'. You use words such as 'always' and 'never', 'nobody' and 'everyone' to make a general rule out of a specific situation.

When you challenge your thinking, ask yourself if you are taking a specific situation and making a general assumption about it. Be sure to turn this back to specific thinking. For example, if you make a mistake, don't tell yourself that you are hopeless, tell yourself that you did not do *that specific thing* as well as usual. If you get rejected, don't tell yourself that you are unlovable, tell yourself that *this particular person* was not right for you.

Reviewing behaviour

Task

We all use distorted thinking patterns at times; it is very common. With that thought in mind, look at what you have already written in your Thought Record.

- Have you made any generalizations about yourself or your behaviour?
- If so, be sure to come up with an alternative thought that is specific.

Mind-reading

This is one of the commonest thinking errors we make when our self-esteem is low. Without someone saying anything to us, we 'know' what they are thinking and why they act the way they do. In particular, we are able to divine how people are feeling towards us. It is fatal to our self-esteem because we think that everyone agrees with our negative opinions of ourselves.

- 'I know he thinks I am boring.'
- 'I can tell she doesn't like me.'
- 'I'm sure they don't really want me in their group.'

Yet we are jumping to conclusions without any real evidence. And for some reason we only seem to have the gift of mind-reading *negative* views; interestingly, we never seem to develop a talent for mind-reading positive thoughts!

Writing such thoughts down in a Thought Record will help you to re-evaluate this supernatural thinking ability and challenge your mind-reading certainties.

Filtering

With this, we take negative details from a situation and then magnify them, at the same time filtering out all the positive aspects. For example: you have dressed beautifully for a formal evening and your partner pays you the well-deserved compliment of saying how nice you look. However, as you leave the room he mentions that the hem of your skirt is not quite straight at the back. You now feel that you no longer look lovely and the evening is spoiled as you worry about the hem of your dress. The fact that, apart from this, you look stunning passes you by.

Polarized thinking

We think of people, situations or events in extremes, such as good or bad: 'I must be perfect or I am a failure', 'If I'm not beautiful, I'm ugly'. There is no middle ground. The problem is that we usually find ourselves on the negative end of our polarized extremes. So if you cannot be perfect, you must be all bad; if you don't get the job you want, your future is ruined; if your relationship doesn't work out, you will never find true love.

Catastrophizing

With this, we expect disaster. We notice or hear about a problem, and start to think 'what if'.

- 'What if tragedy strikes?'
- 'What if it happens to me?'

We then decide that if this terrible thing did happen to us, we would not be able to cope.

Personalizing

This involves thinking that everything people do or say is some kind of reaction to us. For example:

- your partner mentions that the home is looking a little untidy and you immediately 'read' this comment as a criticism of your house-keeping skills
- someone mentions that the work team haven't achieved their targets this month and you instantly decide that this comment is directed at you personally
- you find yourself becoming unnecessarily defensive, and possibly even causing ill feeling, if you take someone's passing remark as personal criticism.

Blaming

This is the opposite of personalization. We hold other people, organizations or even the universe responsible for our problems.

- 'She has made me feel terrible.'
- 'That company ruined my life.'
- 'Life is so unfair.'

We feel unable to change our views or our circumstances, as we see ourselves as victims of other people's thoughtlessness and meanness.

It's all my fault

In this case, instead of feeling a victim, you feel responsible for the pain and happiness of everyone around you.

- If your daughter misses a lift taking her to a special occasion, you feel to blame for not having chivvied her along (even though she is 17 and has taken the whole afternoon getting ready).
- If your firm loses an important client, you will find a way to believe that something you did caused this.

Fallacy of fairness

We feel resentful because we think we know what's fair, but other people won't agree with us. We continually attempt to prove that our opinions and actions are correct. We expect other people to change their views and actions if we pressure or cajole them enough. We try to change people in this way when we believe our hopes for happiness depend entirely on their behaving differently.

Self-assessment ✓

Task

Now you have read through the descriptions of common thinking errors, place a tick by any you feel apply to you.

Generalizing the specific	
Mind-reading	
Filtering	
Polarized thinking	
Catastrophizing	
Personalizing	

Blaming	
It's all my fault	
Fallacy of fairness	

Checking out possible thinking errors is another excellent skill to add to your toolbox. Make sure that you use it regularly. While it can be hard to discover that much of your thinking is biased by negative distortions, acknowledging this is the first step to change. The next step is to use this knowledge to help you with your self-esteem.

Reviewing behaviour

Task

Show a copy of the distorted thinking patterns to family, friends and/ or work colleagues, and ask them if they recognize any that they use themselves. In all probability, they will smile wryly as they admit to most of them! How do you feel, knowing that these are errors most of us make.

Now look through your Thought Record and see if there is one thinking error that you use more than others. Which one?

Chapter summary

What cognitive behavioural therapy (CBT) creates, more than anything else, is *movement*. To feel differently about ourselves, about others, to act differently, to achieve different outcomes, all require us to move away from often long-held beliefs and actions and to be willing to test reality. Is this really true? Does this really matter? Can I change things and if so, how? Most importantly, we need to become curious as to outcomes. Outcomes usually involve how we feel. Whatever happens, we want to feel better about ourselves and CBT is a wonderful mechanism for achieving this.

We have covered the basics in this chapter and now we will move on to further skills to help you to improve your self-esteem. One of the best questions we can ever ask ourselves as we mentally criticize ourselves yet again for not being up to scratch is, 'Where's the evidence?' Read more about this and further skills in Chapter 6.

More tools for challenging self-defeating thoughts

Overview

Now that you have understood the basic tools that CBT offers to promote change and optimism, and help you towards a much higher regard for yourself, we introduce some new skills. If you have ever been into a court of law, you will know that a judge deals in facts only. A judge is not interested in your views – what the court would call 'circumstantial evidence' – but wants only the facts. Were you there, or weren't you? Did you say that, or didn't you? Is that glove yours, or isn't it? Where is the evidence?

In this chapter you will learn to:

- check for evidence
- throw 'should', 'must' and 'ought' out of the window of your rational thinking and to replace them with more helpful and less damning alternatives
- weaken the strength of your negative thoughts and beliefs
- strengthen more balanced alternative ideas that will encourage you to consider yourself in a much better and stronger light
- bring your positive qualities into focus.

Your positive qualities have been there all along, but simply out of your focus. Bringing them back into focus will do wonders for your self-esteem.

Tool 1: Checking for evidence

What goes through you mind when you challenge your Inner Critic and write down more positive, rational alternatives? Many people write diligently, but the thought in their mind is 'I don't really believe this – what I really still believe are the views of my Inner Critic.'

How can you strengthen your belief in your alternative views? One extremely helpful tool, considered by many to be the most important 'thought shifter' around, is to ask a simple question: 'If this is really so, where's the evidence?'

Case study

Jenny was concerned about her job. She had heard that some redundancies were possible at her firm and she started thinking about her own performance and whether her boss might find a reason to get rid of her. The more she thought about it, the more weaknesses she came up with – being late for an important meeting last week, failing to sign up a new client company that had looked promising. Was she losing her grip?

Over lunch with her colleague Sue, Jenny voiced her concerns. Her friend of course asked Jenny why she was coming to this negative conclusion, and Jenny cited what had happened – her 'evidence' for her pessimistic thinking. Sue expressed surprise. 'But Jenny, several people were late for that meeting due to the Tube strike – it couldn't be helped. And though it was disappointing to lose the client, that may not have been your fault at all – you made an excellent presentation, and there were many possible reasons why the client may not have gone ahead. Now think of all the new business you have brought in to the firm this year, which you seem to be discounting.'

In essence, Sue was presenting Jenny with evidence to contradict Jenny's self-defeating thoughts. But Jenny had not thought of this herself, as she was too focused on her negative views of her abilities.

This is what can happen to us when our self-esteem is low. We focus on the negative and ignore the helpful evidence.

Behaviour changing strategy

Task

Practise checking for evidence.

- Look back to your most recent self-critical thought.
- Ask yourself what evidence you had to support it.
- If you were a barrister in a court of law, could you provide evidence against it?
- What would you say?

Giving evidence in your Thought Record

We want you to introduce this element of checking evidence into your Thought Record. In the version of your Thought Record below, you will see that that there are now two extra columns.

The first new column asks you to find evidence to support your Inner Critic's negative comments. For example, if you have looked in the mirror just before going out and thought 'I look dreadful', where is your evidence?

- Is your hair a mess? (Fix it.)
- Are your clothes wrong? (Change them.)
- Or do you just feel low about yourself?

Start with the evidence to support your self-critical thoughts. You will usually find it harder than you think to come up with solid reasoning.

- Would 'Oh, I just do' stand up in a court of law?
- What would a judge think of your evidence?
- Would the judge accept it or throw it out?

The second new column asks you to find evidence to support your alternative thinking. Using the example above, an alternative thought might be 'I really don't look too bad.' It will be easier to believe this if you write in evidence such as:

The full Thought Record

What happened	What you thought when this happened (How strongly do you believe this, on a scale of 1–10?)	How you felt (How strongly did you feel this, on a scale of 1–10?)	Evidence to support your negative thought	Alternative thoughts (Generate at least 2–3 alternatives; rate your belief in them, on a scale of 1–10)	Evidence to support your alternative thoughts	How do you feel now? (Rate any change now you have looked at things more positively)
Example: Failed my driving test	I'll never learn to drive (generalization) (8)	Depressed (8)	After 10 lessons I couldn't pass.	This doesn't mean I'll never pass (6) Many people fail their test first time (6)	My instructor's been very complimentary. My brother failed his test twice and then passed.	A little more optimistic. I will book another test (9)

- 'My partner always tells me I look nice when I get dressed up.'
- 'My best friend has asked to borrow this dress next Saturday.'

As you get used to finding evidence for your alternative thinking, the tangible, logical arguments will loosen your Inner Critic's hold on your mind in a way that simply repeating optimistic alternatives that you don't really believe will not. This is a very powerful skill.

Behaviour changing strategy

Task

Make several copies of the full Thought Record. It is now a very important tool for you. Use it every time your self-esteem plummets, until you begin to find that you automatically challenge your thinking without having to write anything down.

Tool 2: Overcoming the tyranny of 'should', 'must' and 'ought'

A lot of negative, self-defeating thinking comes from using the words 'should', 'must' and 'ought'. These words imply personal failure almost every time we use them. They cause us to make demands on ourselves and suggest that we cannot meet those demands.

- 'I should have known better.'
- 'I should be able to achieve this.'
- 'I shouldn't have done that.'

This is *not* positive thinking. We may think this is positive self-talk, and that we are motivating ourselves by telling ourselves these things. In fact, it is the exact opposite: 'I should be … (polite, charming, clever etc.) and since I am not, I feel badly about myself'.

When our self-esteem is low and we feel sorry for ourselves, these 'shoulds', 'musts' and 'oughts' extend to others: people 'should' be nicer to us; others 'must' consider us when making their plans; colleagues 'ought' to take into account how busy we are before dumping extra work on our desk.

Visualize yourself gathering all of these words up and dropping them into the nearest rubbish bin.

What can we put in their place? Options include:

- acceptance – adopting the idea that it is OK to be fallible ourselves and that others also make mistakes
- replacing 'should', 'must' and 'ought' with softer, less absolute and critical language: 'It would be great if I can achieve this, but it's not the end of the world if I don't'; 'It would have been better if I'd remembered to … but I am as fallible as the next person'.

Behaviour changing strategy

Task

Write down three sentences using 'should', 'must' or 'ought' in a way that relates to negative thoughts that you have or had about yourself in a recent situation.

Now rewrite the sentences leaving out 'should', 'must' or 'ought'.

Did you find that easy or difficult? Practise this a lot and you will find that your confidence will improve as you stop being so hard on yourself and others.

Reviewing behaviour

Task

Focus on how often you use the word 'should', and replace it with a softer option. This should increase your awareness of this thinking error and encourage you to make the change permanent.

Tool 3: Ask a friend

We all tend to be far harder on ourselves than we would be on others in a similar situation. We make allowances for the mistakes of family, friends and colleagues; we understand, for others, that one 'bad step' doesn't make a 'bad person'. Yet when it comes to ourselves, we show no leniency.

An excellent tool for helping ourselves to be more self-accepting is to ask yourself the following.

- If my best friend was feeling this way, rather than me, what would I say to them?
- What evidence would I point out to them to help them see that their pessimistic thought or negative self-assessment was not 100 per cent true?'

The answer you come up with will probably be quite different to your own, negative self-talk. We are always much wiser and more constructive at finding positive qualities in others than we are in ourselves. Use your evidence-gathering skills to prove your point and show how little evidence there is for the self-defeating thoughts that your 'friend' has.

Another good question to ask yourself is: 'Would my best friend agree with my negative views of myself? If not, what might they say about me?'

Most importantly, then ask yourself 'Why would my friend see me differently to the way I see myself?'

Become your own 'best friend'. Use the questions above regularly and you will find that this will really help you to see yourself and your situation in a more positive way.

Reviewing behaviour

Task

Pick three negative aspects of yourself, or events where you feel that you did not come up to scratch (in your own consideration).

- Note them in your diary.
- Now imagine that your best friend is describing these worries to you. Write down exactly what you would tell *them*.

Does this give you a new perspective on your views about yourself?

Starting to undermine negative beliefs

We have already looked at personal beliefs and learned how they can almost slip by unnoticed when we make observations about ourselves. As explained, this is because we tend not to question their validity. Now you need to start doing this.

You may find it hard to move away from pessimistic thinking if your negative beliefs are deeply entrenched. However, you can still learn to replace these beliefs with a more compassionate and positive view of yourself.

As you will remember from earlier in this book, although our day-to-day self-critical thoughts tend to evolve due to specific events, the beliefs we hold about ourselves are absolute: for example, 'I am boring', 'I am hopeless', 'I am unlikeable'. Can you identify any beliefs you may have about yourself that contribute to your low self-esteem? If you find that difficult, try the following.

- Think back to early experiences that encouraged you to think badly about yourself. What conclusions did you come to about yourself based on events in your childhood?
- Think about the things you may do to keep yourself 'safe'. For example, 'I don't socialize much'. Why not? Your answer may help you discover a belief, e.g. 'I am boring', 'I can't talk to people'.

● Look back at the work you are doing with your Thought Record. Do you notice any repeating patterns in the critical way(s) you describe yourself? What negative beliefs about yourself do your negative thoughts reflect?

Tool 4: The downward arrow

If you remain unsure about what is really going on for you, try the excellent **downward arrow** technique. Take any thought from your Thought Record, and apply a downward arrow to it. For example: you have accepted an invitation to a party and are beginning to feel very nervous.

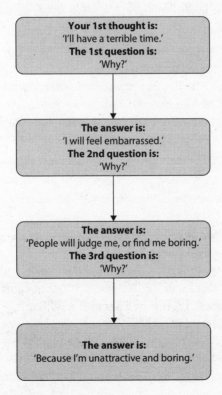

Using this skill, you have uncovered two core beliefs that you have about yourself ('I am unattractive and boring') and which you can now work on. You can also ask yourself another question: 'What is the personal meaning to me if this does or doesn't occur?' Your answer might be: 'I am totally unlikeable'.

Does this make sense to you as a useful, probing technique? Practise it a great deal – it is a vital component in ensuring that you are working on the 'causal' thought or belief (i.e. the thought or belief that is truly responsible for how you are feeling), and not on some superficial idea that won't be relevant to helping you feel better.

Once you have identified any basic self-critical beliefs, you can start to chip away at them and replace them with more helpful and realistic positive beliefs. In this way, your self-esteem and self-acceptance will increase greatly.

Self-assessment ✓

Task

Use the suggestions above to continue to look at self-critical beliefs you may have about yourself. Look especially for beliefs that have been around for a long time.

Where the beliefs come from childhood, recall any particular words of criticism that you may have absorbed.

Replacing old beliefs with new ones

We want you now to begin to focus on your strengths and your good points. Revisit your list of Top Ten qualities and strengths from Chapter 1. Now add a further ten personal qualities.

You may find this difficult, but it is not impossible. Write down your smallest achievements, abilities and personal qualities. We want you to get used to focusing on your *strengths* rather than your *weaknesses*. This is not something you would normally do, so it will not come naturally or easily – all the more reason for doing it!

For example, look at your working day. Whether you are home-based or office-based, there will be plenty of examples on a daily basis of things you are quite good at. Perhaps typing, or cooking, keeping things neat, staying calm when others are getting worked up. Once you start thinking over the last week, you should not find it difficult.

Incorporate things you may like about yourself – 'I am kind', 'I am patient'– as well as things you can do. Don't rate your abilities and qualities. You don't have to be the best at anything before you write it down. Even being quite modest at something counts as a positive: things like 'I don't get too worked up when people are late', 'I managed to stick to my diet for a week' also count.

One of the goals of this exercise is to get you to focus differently. Remember what you have learned: it is not who you are or what happened but your perceptions of who you are or what happened, that define your thinking and your self-esteem. You are now learning to shift your perceptions from negative to positive.

What you have also achieved is to collect a body of evidence to help you ditch your self-critical beliefs. Keep this evidence with you and move on to the next step.

Bringing positive qualities into focus

A simple but very effective tool for questioning self-critical beliefs and bringing positive qualities into focus is a positive data log. Take a negative belief that you hold, and start by finding any evidence you can that might suggest your belief is not true all the time. You can use some of the evidence that you collected previously.

Positive data log

Self-critical belief

_____

_____

New alternative belief

_____

_____

Evidence to support your new belief and weaken your old belief:

1 _____
2 _____
3 _____
4 _____
5 _____
6 _____
7 _____
8 _____
9 _____
10 _____
11 _____
12 _____
13 _____
14 _____
15 _____
16 _____
17 _____
18 _____
19 _____
20 _____

An example might be:

- Self-critical belief: I am unlikeable
- New alternative belief: I am quite likeable

Evidence to support your new belief and to weaken your old belief (showing that the self-critical belief is not true all the time):

1 I do have a few friends.
2 I have been invited to several social occasions so far this year.
3 In general, people are pleasant to me.
4 My work colleagues are friendly.
5 I get invited to workplace social functions.
6 I do my best to be kind and thoughtful.
7 My neighbour thanked me for my helpfulness.
8 I normally have a steady partner, and I have been in two long-term relationships.
9 Although I said 'no', I have received a marriage proposal.
10 I am close to my family.

We have not suggested too big a swing from negative belief to positive belief. Changing beliefs can take several months, so a 'middle of the road' alternative ('I am quite likeable') will serve you better to start with than an unrealistic 'I am totally likeable'.

Reviewing behaviour

Task

Start filling in your positive data log. We suggest you prepare two or three, and gradually add to your evidence for each one over a period of a week or two as you observe events and experiences that support them.

Measuring the strength of new beliefs

Self-critical beliefs take longer to change than our day-to-day, event-specific negative thinking. This is because they have been around a lot longer and are more absolute. However, you will begin to see some change fairly quickly, and you will gain encouragement from using a rating scale to track this. Start by rating the strength of your belief before you start to practise your new skills, and then rate the strength of your belief after a few weeks of practice. Don't expect to see an increase of 100 per cent; that would be unrealistic.

For example, if your original, self-critical belief was 'I am unlikeable' and the belief you would like to replace it with is 'I am likeable most of the time' (note that this is not a total opposite, but a realistic alternative), your rating scale might look like this:

Desired belief: 'I am likeable most of the time'

X				
0%	25%	50%	75%	100%

Strength of belief before two weeks of skills practice

	X			
0%	25%	50%	75%	100%

Strength of belief after two weeks of skills practice

These are subjective ratings, but you will have a good feel for how you are progressing, and by continuing to use your Thought Record and Positive Data Log, you will find that you are gathering more and more evidence to support your new beliefs. You are training your mind to refocus on your more positive characteristics and to re-evaluate the accuracy of your negative beliefs.

Be patient as you work for change. Don't expect overnight success and then give up because of a lack of it. Rating any changes is a helpful way of seeing some improvement – and even if it is only slight, it is a success.

Self-assessment ✓

Task

Rate your self-critical beliefs as you see them now. You may find that, immediately, you don't really want to put your X over the zero. Place it on the scale as accurately as you can.

What does the fact that not all your crosses are on zero tell you about your thinking?

Testing negative predictions

You can use simple, practical experiments to test out negative predictions. For example, Pat believed that she was dull and uninteresting. What sort of assumptions or Rules for Living do you think Pat might have? Perhaps:

- 'If I speak to people they will find out how dull and boring I am' (assumption)
- 'If I keep myself to myself, people won't realize how hopeless I am' (Rule for Living).

Pat was asked to devise some experiments to test out her beliefs, and she came up with the following.

Experiment 1

Make a simple comment to at least ten people, who could include shop assistants, receptionists, the milkman, etc.

Pat's prediction: no one will speak to me; they will think I am odd and I will feel embarrassed.

What actually happened: six people began a conversation with Pat; three people smiled at her; one person ignored her comments.

Experiment 2

Invite a friend to visit the theatre or cinema with you.

Pat's prediction: whoever I ask will make an excuse and I will feel unlikeable.

What actually happened: the first person Pat asked could not come but sounded genuinely disappointed. The second person accepted immediately and thanked Pat for thinking of her.

Experiment 3

At lunch in the staff canteen, ask to sit with different people each day for a week, and note their responses.

Pat's prediction: this will be embarrassing. People will find it hard to say 'no', and I will feel I'm intruding.

What actually happened: on one of the days, the person she asked said they were just leaving the table; on another, the colleagues she chose were engrossed in a work problem and Pat was unable to join in. However, on three of the five days, Pat's colleagues welcomed her and chatted to her with interest. Pat relaxed and actually enjoyed it. Testing things out encouraged Pat to modify her 'I'm dull and boring' belief to one of 'Some people find me quite interesting'. Pat was also able to use her experiments to add to her positive data log. If Pat continues with her experiments, she may be able to modify this belief even further, to, perhaps, 'I appear interesting to most people'.

Testing out negative predictions is an excellent way to challenge negative beliefs. The worst that can happen is that it is as bad as you predict, but you are more likely to find that what happens is quite different from your negative expectations.

Behaviour changing strategy

Task

Devise a small experiment for yourself to test out one of your self-critical beliefs. Make it very simple and easy, so that you are not tempted to duck out. Make a prediction, and measure it against what actually happens.

'Think positively'

Many people suggest that the way to get rid of our Inner Critic is simply to 'think positively'. This is not entirely without merit. It is, however, very difficult to do – if it were easy, we would all feel remarkably good about ourselves all the time, which is not the case.

So how can we restructure 'think positively' to make it more of a concept that might help us? How do we keep our positive qualities in the forefront of our minds? The American psychologist Martin Seligman has come up with an exercise he calls the Three Blessings. Professor Seligman's wide-ranging research in the USA shows empirically that doing this exercise for as little as one week has a very positive effect on our view of ourselves and life generally. The table 'Bringing my positive qualities into focus' is a slightly adjusted (and renamed) version of this that we have produced for the purposes of this book.

There are two reasons this exercise is so effective.

- It's simple – at the end of each day, you write down three positive things that have happened and that were caused by a positive quality of your own. The events may be very insignificant, e.g. The postman smiled at me as I went to work.
- You have to explain – and this is harder – *why* this happened in terms of a positive aspect of yourself, e.g. The postman smiled at me ... because I appear friendly.

Here are some other examples to help you get the idea.

- 'I brought my colleague a cup of coffee', which you might relate to a personal quality such as, 'I am a thoughtful person, at least some of the time.'
- 'I managed to plumb in the dishwasher' ... 'I do have *some* DIY skills'.

Don't be over-modest in your assessments. If you have done anything reasonably OK, allow yourself to feel good about it. Feeling good about yourself is not a crime!

Diary/journal write-in ✏️

Task: Bringing my positive qualities into focus

Make several copies of the chart below so that you can fill it in for at least a week.

(Date)	What happened/ What did I do?	What was the outcome?	What does this tell me that is positive?
1			
2			
3			

Evaluate any changes in your thinking.

Ask yourself why this might be making a difference and what you see as the main purpose of this exercise.

Chapter summary

By the end of this chapter you will have a bulging toolbox of skills to help you overcome and replace your low self-esteem thinking. You have learned:

- to challenge self-critical thinking by asking 'Where's the evidence?'
- to bring your positive qualities more into focus, instead of discounting or dismissing them
- to look for evidence to support your more balanced, optimistic alternative thoughts and beliefs.

It is usual to find far more evidence to support your balanced thoughts than your negative thoughts. This in itself tells you that your thinking is skewed towards the negative and needs to be refocused.

The exercise of noting three positive events every day and why they happened gets your brain used to noticing the positive and happy things instead of dwelling on the negative. It's the mental equivalent of any physical exercise you do – both physical and mental exercise are equally importance, so don't forsake one for the other: do both.

In Chapter 7 we will look at a further skill: being mindful. This means welcoming the present moment and appreciating the 'here and now' rather than letting your brain spend most of its time ruminating on the past or worrying about the future.

Developing mindful awareness

Overview

So far, we have looked at a very active, structured process for enhancing self-esteem. This process has involved identifying and challenging patterns of thinking – making our mind seek more balanced alternatives to our negative views – and then adjusting what we do, working with goal lists and plans of action. From these activities comes the ability to feel much better about ourselves; to see ourselves in a different, more positive light. This is CBT in action, teaching you life skills that will stay with you forever.

A useful addition to these CBT tools is mindfulness. Mindfulness and CBT together provide you with a broader, more comprehensive process for helping you towards good self-esteem. Mindfulness, however, involves a different way of dealing with and processing unhelpful thoughts – no goals, no plans, no actual 'doing' at all. This is called Mindfulness-based CBT, which some readers may have heard of, and some may already practise. For those who are not familiar with this way of being, Chapter 7 helps you to learn more about it.

The actual 'how to' of mindfulness cannot really be taught in one chapter of a book, as it is too complex a process and also something that you need to experience by trying it. The aim of this chapter is to give you an understanding of mindfulness in the hope that you will want to know more and perhaps start to practise it, either in private or at one of the many classes that are now available

The basics of mindfulness

Answer 'yes' or 'no' to the following questions:

- Have you ever sat in a talk or lecture and realized halfway through that you have followed very little of what has been said?
- Do you eat your food quickly, or only glance at the newspaper, or cut short unproductive conversations, so that you can 'get on'?
- Would you say that you regularly have too much to do and suffer from the mental stress of having several 'to do' lists in your head at once?
- Do you pay particular attention to what is going on when you are performing day-to-day tasks, or do you perform them robotically while thinking of other things?
- Do you find it very easy to be judgemental, usually in a negative way?

How many of your answers were 'yes'? Don't berate yourself if you answered 'yes' five times; that is normal. This is what most of us do, most of the time. But do we feel good about ourselves, living this way? Rushing this way and that? Noticing little and enjoying even less?

There is another way; mindfulness. It is not an easy way and you would need to incorporate it into your daily life on a permanent basis to truly benefit from it. It isn't a set of techniques that you can learn and bring out when you need them. Rather, it is a 'way of being' that encourages you to adopt a whole new view of life that will bring you peace and contentment. To this extent, it is hard to master and you must consider it a life-long process – but one you will enjoy.

Practising mindfulness does not in any way inhibit problem-solving brain activity. Its purpose is to do away with ruminative, unhelpful thinking that achieves nothing other than making us feel low or anxious. These 'random thoughts' are rarely about anything special; they are usually negative; they may be critical of others or ourselves; they simply inhabit our brain without any purpose except to keep us divorced from what we are actually doing and any pleasure we might otherwise get from life.

Mindfulness has been validated by science. Neuroscientists measured the difference in individuals' brain patterns before practising mindfulness and again after a period of practice (usually eight weeks), and the results showed that those who practise regularly are calmer and more positive; they think more clearly, do not fight every negative thought and are no longer prey to their brains going round in circles – the 'chatterbox' is quelled. This can also be referred to as 'living in the moment' rather than in the past or the future.

The origins of mindfulness

Mindfulness is a form of meditation originally found in ancient Eastern teachings, but in the past 30 years it has been especially developed by an American psychologist, Jon Kabat-Zinn, who started a mindfulness-based programme at the University of Massachusetts Medical School. Initially intended to help those in chronic pain, it is now widely used to help a variety of problems, including stress, depression and anxiety. Mindfulness has been audited and evaluated and its results are impressive; the NHS now recommends it as a treatment for depression. A large proportion of those who undertake the programme remain stress-free in the long term (provided that they continue to practise what they have learned). Jon Kabat-Zinn called his treatment programme Mindfulness-based Stress Reduction.

In the 1990s, the eminent psychologists Zindel Segal, Mark Williams and John Teasdale studied Kabat-Zinn's programme and used it to develop a further use for mindfulness. They called this Mindfulness-based Cognitive Therapy (MBCT). Both of these therapeutic approaches have become highly popular and courses are widely available.

'Doing' mode

Have you ever done this? You make yourself a cup of tea or coffee, take it with you to your desk or coffee table and take a sip. After a while, you think you'll take another sip and pick up your cup – to find there is no coffee left in it. Without even noticing, you have drunk the lot.

Or you have to drive from A to B, a route you know well. As you drive, your head becomes a chatterbox of thoughts and concerns. Before you know it, you have arrived at place B. Can you recall anything about your journey at all? Did you see any squirrels, children playing, cars with new number plates etc? No, of course not. You weren't paying attention to the present moment. You were living in your head, making your lists, going through how much you had to do before next Thursday, how to tell your wife that you had a crucial work presentation on school sports day, and so on.

There is nothing wrong with this. We all do it most of the time. But we are missing the present moment. In mindfulness terms, we are in 'doing' mode rather than 'being' mode.

We are in 'doing' mode when our brain is constantly trying to resolve a problem. This may be conscious, such as 'How will I find the time to complete my project?', or unconscious, such as walking from home to the park when the brain is working all the time to figure out what needs to be done – put one foot in front of the other, walk this way, turn left there, get closer to your end destination. Your brain is working on your behalf all the time.

The brain's natural propensity is to look at two positions: Position A is where you are now, and Position B is where you would like/need to be. This can be in terms of geography or in terms of work promotions, relationships, or even cooking the dinner. The brain's task is to help you to narrow the gap between A and B, until B is achieved. This is the brain's 'doing' mode. Unfortunately, 'doing' mode can be tiring and stressful and doesn't always give us the solutions we want, which can make us feel more stressed and hopeless. We berate ourselves in 'doing' mode. We beat ourselves up, admonish stupid actions, focus on our weaknesses – in short, we work hard at developing our low self-esteem. This is not to decry 'doing' mode. We need to be active and to be problem-solvers. But we also need to know when to switch off: when 'doing' mode becomes unhelpful and when it stops us enjoying life.

'Being' mode

In the words of Jon Kabat-Zinn, 'Mindfulness means paying attention in a particular way: on purpose, in the present moment and non-judgementally.' This is 'being' mode. It is the opposite of driven, goal-oriented 'doing' mode, relentlessly trying to reduce the gap between how things are and how we would like them to be. The focus of 'being' mode is on accepting and allowing things to be how they are without immediately going into the more pressured 'how do I change this?' way of thinking.

As in all things, there is a time and a place for 'being' mode. It is not about learning to put everything permanently to one side while you live your life accepting all that it going on around you. It is about being able to find time within your day, your week, your life, to relieve the stress, to move away from your low mood, and to be calmly and non-judgementally present in the moment, aware of your experiences and calmly paying attention.

The benefits of being mindful

One answer to the question 'What do we get from being mindful?' is the somewhat frustrating 'Whatever it means to you'. It is true that mindfulness isn't in any way about solving problems: it truly is just a way of being, and this experience is individual to each of us. Practitioners may even say that it cannot be written about but only experienced. The emphasis on experiential learning is because of this individual benefit. It is what it is for *you*. You will get a great deal from it. But it will take time and come gradually, and how you feel personally may be different to anyone else.

Less abstract answers to the question of what we get from being mindful would be:

- it increases awareness. Mindfulness will help you to notice in a positive way the sights and sounds around you. You will become more aware of everything you see, hear, smell, etc. You will be aware of where you are, how you feel – you will be in the present moment.
- it relaxes your body and enables you to get back in touch with it.
- it creates a calmer mind by taking a step back from your thoughts and ruminations, the main goal of most people who try mindfulness.
- it reduces pain. If you suffer from physical pain, mindfulness can help to reduce it. Many people who have 'tried everything' have found mindfulness to work when nothing else did.
- it enables you to stand away from your thoughts without blocking them; 'That which we resist, persists' so we cannot block out our thoughts, but we can learn to stand back and observe them without them swamping us. This enables us to evaluate them better, appreciating that they are just thoughts, not truths. When we do this, our painful, critical thoughts will soften and glide away on their own.
- your mind becomes more attentive to the present moment, which helps you to focus better and become a better decision maker. It calms the thoughts in your head that prevent you from fully absorbing what is happening, be it a workplace presentation, a junior school play, etc.
- mindfulness helps you understand and calm your emotions. Often, our emotions become so strong that they 'take over' and we lose the ability to think clearly or to respond in the best way to something. Mindfulness helps to reduce and eliminate these possibilities, and helps you to manage your feelings.
- mindfulness meditation helps you to see things in a better perspective.
- mindfulness helps you to learn to be at peace with yourself.

Practising mindfulness

Mindfulness is achieved by practising on a daily basis a variety of meditation and breathing techniques that train your body and your mind to become accustomed to this new, stress-free, present state of being.

A variety of books on mindfulness are available that describe meditations for you to follow, or there are CD sets in which a mindfulness teacher guides you towards how best to meditate and follows the meditation through with you. The most recommended approach, however, would be to take a course. A delightful experience in itself, on a course you can share your experiences with others in a safe and peaceful environment.

Courses usually follow similar formats, running for eight weeks with two hours of tutored experiential work each week, followed by approximately one hour's practice each day at home; and towards the end of the course one full day of tuition to practise for a longer period the various new ways of being that you have learned. Wherever you live, it should be possible to find a course in basic Mindfulness-based Stress Reduction (MBSR) or Mindfulness-based Cognitive Behavioural Therapy (MBCBT).

Behaviour changing strategy

Task: Mindful breathing

If you wish to try mindfulness at home, this is a short, simple daily meditation practice to start you off. It will take about ten minutes, so make sure that you have the time to give to it and that you will not be interrupted.

1 Find somewhere comfortable to sit or lie down. You can sit in a chair or cross-legged on the floor – whichever you feel will help you to focus best. If you lie down, lie flat on your back with your legs straight. Try to keep your spine straight. If you are sitting, imagine that that a string from the top of your head is being pulled gently upwards; in other words, don't slouch!Remember, the experience is simply

whatever it is for you from moment to moment. You are not striving to achieve anything, to reach a goal. Just be still, with things as they are, in the present moment.

2 Begin to focus on your breathing and any sensations this creates. Be aware of the bodily movements involved in breathing: how your nostrils flare slightly, how your stomach rises and falls, how your breath moves round your body. Try to keep your focus of attention on your breathing. Notice any parts of your body where sensation arises, however slight. This will also help to keep you focused.

You will almost certainly find that your mind begins to wander after a while. You may not notice it at first but at some point you will have an awareness of your wandering thoughts. This is fine; don't worry about it – 'wandering off' is what minds do and is all part of the meditation process; you will gradually 'wander off' for shorter periods before you become aware of what is happening – just guide your thoughts back to your breath. Leave any intrusive thoughts to their own devices, i.e. don't get into conversation with them, and you will find that they will soften and gradually disappear of their own accord.

3 Continue this breathing meditation for ten minutes or thereabouts (use a timer or an alarm if you would like to be exact) and then gently open your eyes. As you become practised at this mediation, you can increase the time you spend on it to 15 minutes and then to 20 minutes if you wish.

You may be curious about how you are 'supposed' to feel at the end of this starter meditation: what are you 'supposed' to get out of it? The answer is that you have made a start at learning to 'be' rather than to 'do', so well done! Be willing to accept whatever arises, good or bad, and keep practising. My hope for you, though, is that you will have felt peaceful and calm at the end of your meditation. Although mindfulness is, in essence, without goals, my aims for you are that, over a period, you will find it much easier to:

- accept negative, distressing thoughts and feelings but no longer join in a conversation with them
- discover that the platform you have built for your awareness of the present is strong enough for you to invite your mind to join you in this sense of peace.

If you find meditation difficult, use shorter time periods until you find the length of time that is right for you. Then extend the time as you become more comfortable with the meditation process. Remind yourself that boredom is part of life: continue your meditation and notice whether the boredom passes once you have accepted it. Also consider trying guided mediation with a CD or download an app such as 'Simply Being'. You may be better able to keep your mind in the moment with the focus of spoken guidance.

Practice advice ⇨

Being mindful in everyday life

Here are some suggestions for being mindful in a simple way in your everyday life. If you do nothing more than this, you will still be helping yourself to become calmer and more at peace with yourself.

- From the moment you wake up, and throughout the day, take the time occasionally to pay attention to your breathing for a short while. Focus fully on your breathing for a few moments and then return to what you were doing. Notice as well any bodily sensations and take a moment to examine them.
- Start eating and drinking mindfully. Take time over your food. Chew it well: savour and enjoy it; focus on it (don't read a book at the same time, for example). Do the same with any drink you are given or make for yourself. Be present with your food and drink and focus on the pleasure it gives you.
- When you are walking anywhere, be aware of your posture, how your body feels, what muscles you are using and stretching. Focus on this rather than the thoughts buzzing round in your head.
- Ensure that any journeys you make by car or other transport are 'mindfully' taken. Give yourself a target, such as five things that you will notice on your journey that bring a smile to your face: children playing; a squirrel in a tree; someone proudly driving a new car. Be aware of your journey. As with the breathing meditation, if you find your thoughts wandering, bring them back to the moment and renew your awareness of the here and now.

- When you find yourself feeling impatient or frustrated, return your mind to your breathing. Attempt to let go of any judgements you are making; simply be aware of what is happening in an impartial way.
- Be as kind as you can, both to yourself and to others. Mindfulness generates warmth and compassion. It is non-judgemental. It is a better way to be, and as you practise you will find it easier. Learn to forgive yourself for being a fallible human being and accept yourself as you are.
- Finally, as you settle into bed at night, focus on your breathing for a few minutes. Be aware of how your breathing slows when you focus on your abdomen rising and falling and when you are present in the moment rather than wandering off into the hinterlands of stressful thinking.

A personal mindfulness tip

Focus on listening to sounds. When I wake up in the morning, this is what I do for a few minutes. I may hear birdsong, or rain hitting the windows, breezes rustling in the trees, car engines, or occasionally sirens, in the distance. Or the creaking sound of someone else in the house opening a door, rustling a newspaper, or the sounds of a kettle coming to the boil. For me, this is an easy way to be mindful and a very calming process.

Chapter summary

In this chapter you have learned:

- the concept of mindfulness
- how mindfulness may offer positive effectiveness in your life
- a simple mindfulness exercise.

You now understand mindfulness well enough to consider taking it further, either through more reading, listening to CDs, or perhaps taking a course. (See the Further reading section.)

You have perhaps tried a brief mindfulness meditation for yourself. At the start, these can be confusing as most people have a sense of 'I should be getting something specific from this'. You will, but it is gradual. Inner peace takes time and practice. Begin to incorporate mindful ways into your everyday life. As mindfulness becomes a habit it becomes easier and the release of stress eventually becomes visible.

PART 3

Escape

Confront negative thoughts and behaviours and begin to replace them with new ones

CHAPTER 8

Empowerment: the freedom of taking responsibility

Overview

In this chapter we will look at 'stuckness'. When we want to feel more confident and are eager to do so, what prevents this? Often, it is that we are not taking enough personal responsibility for our negative thoughts and feelings. Just as we may look to other people or specific situations to encourage our good self-esteem, we often also look externally to 'blame' other people or impossible situations for our upset feelings. The problem with this is that it leaves us unable to move on. If it's not our fault, how can we change anything? This chapter will teach you how.

Negative disempowerment

How you perceive what goes on around you, and how you interpret your abilities to deal with things has a great impact on self-esteem.

Case study

Sara was in a troubled relationship, and her partner, James, had recently moved out of their shared home. Although James had treated her cruelly on occasion, having several affairs and behaving in a moody and erratic way, Sara's self-esteem was so low that she interpreted his behaviour as a response to her own hopelessness and unlovability.

Sara spent a lot of time telephoning and emailing James, begging him to come home. She felt that, without him, she was totally unlovable, and that she needed him desperately to restore her confidence. In the end, James reluctantly agreed to Sara's pleading and returned home. However, the relationship continued to deteriorate, as James did not really want to be there and continued to see other women.

Sara's despair came from feeling absolutely stuck. She felt she had tried as hard as she could in the relationship and that it was James' cruel treatment that made her feel so badly about herself.

If only James would change, she would feel OK about herself again. Without his input, Sara felt unable to deal with her life.

We can feel completely stuck when we disempower ourselves in this way, with thoughts such as 'I feel so badly due to someone else's behaviour, and need them to change in order to feel better'. We do sometimes receive an increase in our personal 'feel-good factor' when people treat us well, but we cannot rely on this. The moment we say, 'If he had not done that, I would not have felt this way', 'I only acted that way because of the way she behaved', or 'If she would only treat me with more respect, I'd feel so much better', we are trapped in a way of thinking that prevents us from taking responsibility and making changes.

You will suffer from low self-esteem forever if you blame anyone else for making you feel the way that you do. You may be right – so-and-so may be rude, may have run you down terribly, may have landed you in it, made you look a fool, or whatever – but it is not about what other people do; it is how you respond to what they do that decides whether you feel helplessly disempowered or not.

Self-assessment ✓

Task

Think about the last time someone let you down in some way, e.g. by cancelling an engagement at the last minute.

- Did you feel a victim? In other words, did you feel that the actions of the other person were to blame for how you felt?
- Was this a 'one-off' or do you often feel this way?
- What might you do differently the next time it happens?

Personalization

We looked briefly at personalization in Chapter 1. Having done so, would you now find it easier to identify any recent situations when you may have fallen into this trap yourself? Here are some examples.

- Somebody makes a comment about liking long hair, and you immediately think they are criticizing your new short cut.
- Your boss tells you that the department is lagging behind in completing an important project on time and you assume he is commenting on your performance.
- You suggest to your friend or partner that you get takeaway pizzas tonight, and they pull a face and say, 'No, I really don't fancy pizza.' What you hear is: 'What a rotten choice – can't you think up anything better than that?'

When you personalize, you erroneously feel that you are personally to blame for the perceived negative reactions of others: 'If someone disagrees with me, I must be wrong, and that makes me stupid'. You must identify these thoughts and counteract them. This involves using some of the broader thinking skills we discussed in earlier chapters, such as the following.

- Having respect for the opinions of others, as you hope they will respect yours. You are not stupid if you disagree with them, just as they are not if they disagree with you.
- Distinguishing between opinion and fact. However strongly either you or the person talking to you believe something, that doesn't make it true. There are many different opinions on most subjects. Opinions are exactly that – simply points of view.

- Have confidence in your own views. You don't need to be right all the time – just having a view shows thoughtful intelligence on your part, and you may have valid reasons/past experiences that mean you are more likely to have formed your opinions in a certain way.
- Others have their own problems. Your boss may have been under a lot of pressure from his superior to get this work out, and the friend who didn't want pizza may have been preoccupied with a relationship difficulty.
- Other people don't always react in the best possible way. This has nothing to do with you.

Start being much more aware of over-personalizing the comments of others, and use your thinking skills to review the situation. Remember, comments are not always criticism, and criticism isn't always personal.

Self-assessment ✓

Task

Think back over the recent past to an occasion when you might have erroneously taken something too personally.

- What went through your mind?
- How strongly did you believe it? (Rate how strong your belief was on a scale of 1–10, where 10 = fine.)
- Consider some alternative ways of thinking about this, using some of the skills mentioned above.
- How do you feel now? (On a scale of 1–10, where 10 = fine).

Self-pity

Every time you run yourself down, you are indulging in self-pity. Self-pity is similar to getting locked into victim mode, except on this occasion you are not blaming others as much as you are blaming yourself – and feeling sorry for yourself.

Thoughts typical of self-pitying thinking are:

- Why do bad things always happen to me?
- Why am I such an idiot?
- I'll never be any good.
- I always draw the short straw.
- I can't get anything right.
- I got a bad deal on good looks.

You are allowing your Inner Critic free rein, and not even arguing. It is easier to say 'poor me' and leave it at that. Don't!

We all have 'wallowing' periods. You are allowed these occasionally. But use them wisely, sparingly, and be aware that you are choosing to do so. This will give you breathing space to pull yourself together and look at what you are doing.

Self-pity is:

- destructive – self-pity is destructive because it robs us of an opportunity to make changes. It can also lead to depression. What could be more likely to take you into dark despair than the idea that everything is against you and that there is nothing you can do about it?
- unattractive – others may feel sorry for us, but they may also think we are being self-absorbed and poor company. They may consider us to be negative pessimists, someone to be avoided.
- a waste of energy – the energy that we waste feeling sorry for ourselves could be better spent in problem-solving. Self-defeating worry is physically exhausting, without serving any useful purpose.
- prevents us from moving on – self-pity gives us an excuse to indulge our 'stuckness'. We lose ourselves in self-oriented thoughts instead of action-oriented thoughts, and nothing positive happens: we stay where we are.

Catch self-pitying thoughts as soon as you can. If you need a little 'wallowing' time, that is fine, but limit it and then become constructive. Don't waste energy.

Self-assessment

Task

When did you last feel sorry for yourself?

- Why?
- Do you still feel that way? If not, why not?
- What did you do to stop your self-pitying thoughts?
- How did you feel once they had disappeared?

Taking responsibility for your feelings

One of the easiest ways to get rid of feelings of victimization or self-pity is to take responsibility for ourselves. It is not difficult. Look in the mirror and say this:

'I now take full responsibility for my happiness.'

Now say this:

'No one except myself is responsible for my happiness.'

There you go! Or perhaps you don't; I do appreciate that it is not quite this easy, but it *almost* is.

Case study

Jim was walking down the corridor at work when a colleague coming the other way jostled him, resulting in hot coffee being spilt over Jim's new suit. Instead of apologizing, the colleague made a weak joke about it and rushed on, calling back to Jim that he was late for a meeting but that Jim should send him the bill for the dry-cleaning. Jim was furious. He was left to clean up the mess and dry himself off, and then had to walk into a meeting looking a wreck. In response to a jokey comment made by someone in the meeting concerning his appearance, Jim hit the roof, and was asked by the chairman to leave the room and calm down. Jim's anger had taken over. He blamed his colleagues for his wretched day and for the anger it had produced that seemed to alienate him from several of them.

Was he right? As I am sure you realize, the only person responsible for Jim's anger was Jim himself.

Behaviour changing strategy

Task

Using the skills you have been learning, note down some alternative ways the two people in the case studies above, Sara and Jim, might have dealt with the situations they found themselves in so that better outcomes were achieved. What specific skills might they have used – for example, how else could they have viewed their situations – and what different actions could they have taken? What outcome might they have achieved had they taken a more balanced approach to their problems?

No one else can make you feel anger or any other emotion. You choose to feel that way – and you can choose not to. Engrave on your heart, 'I am responsible for and decide how I react. No one else.'

Once we realize that no one else has control over how we feel – and that we have control over how we feel – we can put the lid on negative emotions. You don't have to. If you wish to be angry or upset, be angry or upset. But acknowledge that you are *choosing* to do so, so make these choices through valid thinking, not hiding behind the excuse 'I couldn't help it'.

With the exception of reflex actions, such as a knee jerk or blushing, we can control our responses. It may be hard, but it can be done. This is called emotional intelligence, which means that we are able to identify and manage our emotions so that we use them appropriately, rather than letting inappropriate emotions take charge of our thinking and actions, which can lead to upset both for ourselves and others and lower our sense of self-worth.

Managing negative emotions

Have you noticed how certain people, who have very little materially in life, seem happy and fulfilled, full of laughter, surrounded by friends, while wealthier people may complain about the unfairness of life and spend a lot of time detailing all what is wrong with their situations?

How can we account for what seem to be discrepancies in how well people do or how happy they are? The answer is **emotional intelligence**, a way of understanding the emotions of ourselves and others and learning to control these emotions so that we are able to choose what we say and what we do, to engender the outcome that we would like to see.

'It's not my fault'

How often do we hear someone say, 'I just couldn't help it' or 'It was completely outside my control' when referring to their actions or verbal responses in a difficult situation? In fact, we can always 'help it', and there is very little that we do where we are not in some sort of control. The difference between someone who uses emotional intelligence and someone who does not is that the emotionally intelligent person will fight to maintain control of his/her emotions and refuse to allow the other person to dictate his/her actions unless appropriate. The person not using emotional intelligence will give way to their emotions regardless of the outcome that results from this (and then say 'I couldn't help it. It just happened.').

Wishing you had done things differently

How many times in your life have you either thought or said, 'I wish I hadn't said that?' or 'I wish I had reacted differently'? The answer is probably more times than you can count, and that is normal for most of us. Becoming emotionally intelligent will reduce the number of times you will find yourself either thinking or saying such things in future.

Here are what many regard as the key skills of emotional intelligence; they are also all key skills for good self-esteem:

- self-awareness: knowing what you are feeling and why
- self-regulation: being able to control your emotions, even when circumstances are difficult
- motivation: being able to persist in the face of discouragement
- empathy: being able to read and identify emotions in others
- social skills: being able to get along with others through listening, understanding and appreciating their emotions.

Developing emotional intelligence will equip you to make choices and influence outcomes in all areas of your life in which you choose to use this skill. The following will help you to understand these ideas a little more.

- Identifying emotions. Emotions contain information, so we need to be able to accurately identify emotions, both in ourselves and in others, to express ourselves well and communicate effectively.
- Using emotions. How we feel influences how we think and what we think about. Emotions direct our attention to important events, ensure that we are ready to take action when required and enable us to use our thoughts appropriately to solve the problem.
- Understanding emotions. Emotions are not random events – they have underlying causes. Once we know what these are, we can use our emotions to understand what is going on, or is about to go on, more easily.
- Managing emotions. Emotions influence our thinking, so we need to incorporate them intelligently into our reasoning and problem-solving. This requires us to be open to emotions, whether they

are welcome or not, decipher what they are telling us, and then choose plans and actions that consider what our feelings are telling us.

Self-assessment ✓

Task

Think about the last time you were in a slightly difficult situation. Did you feel that you handled it well emotionally? If not, spend a moment replaying it in your mind. Which of the characteristics we have been discussing did you lack – and why?

Case study

The queue at the supermarket checkout was getting longer and longer. Margaret, around eighth in line, could not quite see what was happening but when a supervisor was called and the cash register was opened up for investigation, she knew she was in for a long wait. She did feel irritated, but rationalized that there was little she could do and that it was certainly not the cashier's fault. So, smiling resignedly at the person behind her in the queue, she picked a magazine off the rack beside her and started to flick through it. After a few minutes, she became aware of shouting a little further up the queue. Someone near the front was throwing a wobbly at what he termed 'the sheer incompetence and stupidity' of the cashier and supervisor: 'Can't you put this right? Can't you see how huge the queue is? I have to get to an appointment. This is outrageous.' The cashier and supervisor apologized, explained that the till had jammed, which was outside their control, and that they were trying to rectify the problem, and suggested the man go to an alternative till. This led to more shouting: 'Why should I do that? It will lead to even more waiting. This is ruining my evening. I'll never shop here again. I'll be writing to your management about this.' With that, the man left his trolley full of goods and stalked off.

A minute or two after he had left, three things happened. Another cashier opened the till next to the defective one especially for the customers waiting in that queue; the jammed till came back into operation again; and the supervisor gave Margaret and the others in her queue a £5 store voucher as an apology for the disturbance. Margaret was delighted – not only had she got a discount on her shopping, but she had picked up two good recipe ideas from the magazine and had a brief, friendly chat with the lady waiting behind her, discovering that they both played badminton at the same club and arranging to meet up again. She thanked the cashier profusely and got a grateful smile back. Margaret left the store thinking how well things work out sometimes.

Meanwhile, the angry man had no shopping, no voucher, was riled up and angry with the people he was meeting, recounting his 'horrendous' experience, slept very badly and woke up with a headache.

Reviewing behaviour

Task

Which of the characteristics of emotional intelligence listed above are demonstrated in this story, and by whom? Think about this yourself for a moment before reading on.

Margaret was able to recognize her irritation and acted to defuse it: empathizing with the situation instead of being angry about it, distracting herself with a magazine, and having a brief social chat. Meanwhile, the man ahead of her was completely unable to control his emotions and had little, if any, social skills at all. This is an example of emotional intelligence, and the effect it can have on our daily lives. Put simply, emotional intelligence is the ability to get along with both yourself and with others. Learn to take emotional responsibility by being emotionally intelligent. You will feel much better for it.

Don't give up

Giving up can take you back into disempowerment mode.

- 'It's too hard.'
- 'I don't have time.'
- 'It doesn't make sense.'
- 'It doesn't work.'

Dr Robert Anthony (1979) cites research that shows it takes approximately 21 days to break an old, destructive habit or form a new, positive habit. Please keep this in mind. It may take you at least that long to gain positive benefits from what you do. Although you may readily understand the principles of this book, acting on them is harder. You may read a section and say 'I know that', but actually you don't *really* know it. In order to *really* know it, it must become part of your thinking, your emotions, your actions and reactions. Unless this is the case, reading something and understanding it is not enough. Determine to give your new habits, thinking and behaviours time to develop. About 21+ days – and that is working hard!

Self-assessment

Task

In the past year, what have you given up, and why? Write these things down and think about each one in turn. There will no doubt be good and valid reasons for some, but not for all.

- When have you used any of the negative thoughts mentioned above?
- Do you have any regrets about some of the things you have given up?
- How has this affected your self-esteem.

What do you learn from this?

Taking responsibility for your self-development

To obtain the greatest benefit, read through this book in its entirety. Then go back to the sections that deal with specific problems you know you have trouble with. Ensure that you understand where you have been going wrong and how you can put things right. Most importantly, *act* on them.

This is about taking responsibility for your development. This is how you will increase your self-esteem. Don't make excuses: that is what victims do – don't go back into the 'I couldn't help it' style of thinking. You can. You will. And you will succeed.

Chapter summary

In this chapter you have learned:

- the importance of taking responsibility for who we are and how we view ourselves and others
- that falling into 'victim' mode and blaming others contributes to our low self-esteem and can cause us to become completely stuck
- that learning to understand and manage our emotions (emotional intelligence) can help us avoid becoming stuck in negativity
- that a major reason people don't change – or not as much as they want to – is that they give up.

It is natural to hope that when you open a self-help book, a sprinkle of fairy dust will fall out onto you to make everything OK, or that reading it once will 'do the trick'. But, like everything else, it is practice that is the key to change and improvement.

In Chapter 9 we are going to look at a new concept, that of acceptance. This may sound like nothing new, but in relation to our view of ourselves and our views about others, we don't often employ this excellent skill. We waste time and energy *not* accepting who we are and how we behave: we beat ourselves up, are filled with regrets, go over and over our mistakes. How much easier to learn to accept all these things and let the critical thoughts disappear.

CHAPTER 9

Self-acceptance and other-acceptance

Overview

In this chapter we will look at an excellent tool for becoming more comfortable with yourself and liking yourself as you are. Many of us (and I do recall thinking in this way myself when I was in my twenties and more interested in trying to impress people) feel that we need 'add-ons' to make people like us more. Perhaps becoming a good pianist or club tennis champion, taking a job you may not especially like because it has an impressive title and will 'sound good', reading rather dull newspaper articles because you feel that if you can make informed comments others will admire you. Does this sound like you at all? It certainly sounds rather how I used to be! Then I discovered how much better it was to be able to:

- feel OK just being who you are
- know that it's fine to be fallible
- appreciate that others like you more for your character than your achievements.

Self-acceptance will give you all this.

Developing self-acceptance

The work you have done so far has required you to look squarely at your negative thoughts and behaviours and to dispute these: to challenge their truth, to look at alternatives and to check the evidence to support (in most instances) more balanced thinking.

Self-acceptance is a different approach. Instead of arguing with your negative thoughts, you consider them as possibly realistic and truthful – and you may even agree with some them. Your argument against this might be 'But that is what I am doing *now*, which is why I feel so badly about myself!' However, it is not, quite. What is happening now is that when you acknowledge that you may have faults and weaknesses, you do two things (though you may not notice yourself doing them, as it's part of your habitual thinking):

- you generalize the specific; for example, you decide that, as you don't have a scintillating wit, you are a boring person
- you decide that having this weakness is totally unacceptable, resulting in feelings of shame and low self-esteem.

Self-acceptance enables you to conquer your Inner Critic by saying: 'That's fine. I don't mind about these particular things I am no good at. I can accept my shortcomings without diminishing myself.' If you can learn to do this with calm, inner peace and even a little humour, the results can be spectacular.

The secret is for us to stop seeing ourselves as a single entity. We are made up of hundreds of component parts – our skills, abilities, physique, sporting or artistic leanings, levels of competitiveness, intelligence, emotional maturity, personal qualities such as kindness, compassion, generosity or meanness, good or poor humour, etc. If we rate ourselves on each of these strengths and weaknesses individually, we would have very varied ratings; some might be eight or nine out of ten, others just one or two. If we added up the grand total of individual ratings, the figure we end up with would probably be similar to most other people, even though our areas of strength and weakness might be totally dissimilar. We have to stop generalizing the specific. Burning the sausages does not mean you are no good at cooking. It just means that, on this occasion, you burnt the sausages.

Why self-acceptance

Many people find the idea that they can accept themselves, warts and all, and not stay plunged in low self-esteem a paradox. If you already think you are a loser, then surely accepting this is simply throwing in the towel? It depends. That is *unhealthy* self-acceptance. Healthy self-acceptance differs from this in several important ways.

- Healthy self-acceptance encourages you to accept specific weaknesses about yourself, while at the same time rejecting the idea that having these weaknesses makes you an overall no-hoper. People suffering from depression tend to have an unhealthy lack of self-acceptance, and see themselves as generally worthless. A more optimistic personality will reflect only on specific areas of weakness, and not see these weaknesses as meaning that they are not up to scratch in general terms.

- Someone with unhealthy self-acceptance will consider their weaknesses untenable, and revert to the idea of global uselessness. Healthy self-acceptance embraces acknowledging your weaknesses but not writing yourself off because of them. You understand that it is OK to have skills deficits, make mistakes, get things wrong, not have the strengths of the next person. You say: 'This is called being human, as we all are' and you retain your self-respect.

- Unhealthy self-acceptance does not encourage change. It allows its followers to stay as they are, lost in self-criticism and low self-esteem. Their ideas conform to the view that there is no point in trying when failure is a certainty. Or they are 'all talk'; the diet, exercise regime or study course starts tomorrow, but tomorrow never comes. Healthy self-acceptance gives you energy and motivation to change and pursue personal growth. Accepting weaknesses does not mean retaining weaknesses. Change is seen as positive, and accepting your shortcomings without any loss of self-esteem will enable you to meet the challenges change brings.

Self-assessment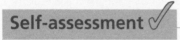

Task

Write down three or four of your perceived personal weaknesses in the table below. For each one, ask yourself two questions:

1 Does having this weakness make me a useless/bad/insignificant person?
2 Am I doing anything towards improving this weakness.

Circle YES or NO.

Weakness	Q1 response	Q2 response
1	YES / NO	YES / NO
2	YES / NO	YES / NO
3	YES / NO	YES / NO
4	YES / NO	YES / NO

Answering 'Yes' to Question 1 and 'No' to Question 2 means you have unhealthy self-acceptance.

Answering 'No' to Question 1 and 'Yes' to Question 2 means you have healthy self-acceptance.

Understanding self-acceptance

Here is a question for you. Is a zebra a black animal with white stripes, or a white animal with black stripes? Write your answer down. We'll come back to this at the end of this chapter.

Now complete the next exercise.

Self-assessment ✓

Task

Look at the big 'I' in the box below. For the purposes of this exercise, this is you! It represents everything about you that makes your totality as a human being.

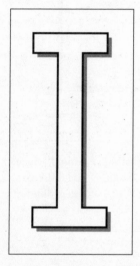

Draw a larger scale version of the big 'I' on a piece of paper.

Think about the qualities that you have, ones that you are aware of yourself or that your family and friends might consider to be your good points, such as knowing a lot about garden plants. For each of these qualities, place a small 'i' inside the big 'I'.

Now think about your weaknesses, again both those that you perceive in yourself and those your family and friends might consider you to have, such as being a poor timekeeper. Place a small 'i' inside the big 'I' for each of these.

What about neutral aspects of yourself? For example, you dress reasonably well, aren't especially overweight, etc. Place a small 'i' in the big 'I' for each of these.

Once you have done all this, your Big I should look like the illustration below.

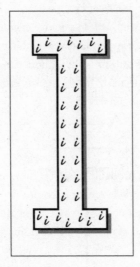

Of all the weaknesses that came to mind, which one currently bothers you the most? Which one makes you dislike yourself the most, feel ashamed of yourself and wish you were different? Circle one little 'i' to represent this.

Look again at your big 'I' – yourself. The little 'i's within it are the sum total of yourself as a human being – good, bad, neutral, warts and all. The circled aspect is just one of many – of hundreds, if you spent much time working on this.

So does this mean you are a good person or a bad person? A success or a failure?

What did you learn from the big 'I', little 'i' exercise? We hope you will have gathered that you are far too complex an individual to be able to rate yourself in just one way. This is the principle of self-acceptance – you learn not to rate or evaluate yourself, but to appreciate that you are made up of hundreds of different facets that are constantly changing and defy any sort of generalized, global assessment of yourself.

This does not mean, however, that you cannot rate individual aspects of yourself. Indeed, self-acceptance encourages this, as doing so allows you to consider whether you would like to make changes and improvements to these aspects – but without running yourself down for having these weaknesses in the first place. For example, perhaps you could improve your timekeeping?

Fallibility

We are *all* fallible. We probably make far more mistakes in life than we accept or acknowledge, or even notice. Many of us keep repeating the same mistakes again and again. This doesn't make us bad people, or idiots; it makes us fallible human beings – in other words, *normal*.

The zebra

How did you get on with the question of the zebra? What did you decide? Did it seem impossible to come up with a definite answer? How might that fit in with our present discussion? Could it mean that it is as difficult to say something is either black or white as it is to say that we are personally useless or perfect, nasty or nice, hopeless or wonderful? The answer to this is almost certainly 'Yes'.

You will recall previous references to challenging assumptions and finding different ways of thinking about things. The question of the zebra illustrates this beautifully. What about this for an answer? 'The zebra is neither a black animal with white stripes, nor a white animal with black stripes, but a pink animal with black and white stripes.'

Fallibility is human. It is fine. It is normal. It simply makes you the same as everyone else. Never stop looking for an alternative way of thinking about things!

Reviewing behaviour

Task

Write down two or three weaknesses that you would like to fix. In the light of what we have learned:

- how badly do you feel about having these weaknesses (on a scale of 1–10, where 1 = very bad, 10 = fine)?
- do you think you have been kinder to yourself with these ratings than you might have been before you had read this chapter on self-acceptance?

We hope that by now you can accept the idea that you do not have a particular global rating as a human being. Rather, you are (as we all are) made up of a huge number of different qualities and characteristics, some of which are strengths, some neutral and some weaknesses. We hope this has helped you see yourself in a more accepting light.

Here are more basic illustrations to ensure you are thinking on the right lines. Consider the following.

The bowl of fruit

Picture a bowl of fruit with all your favourites in it – apples, oranges, pears, grapes, peaches – whichever you like best. Look at the bowl closely. There's a bad fruit in there: a grape with mould, or an apple with a worm-hole. What will you do? Throw the whole bowl of fruit away, or just throw away the mouldy grape or wormy apple and keep the rest? If the latter, then why write yourself off as a person rather than accepting or working on the individual weakness?

The green frog

Imagine that, when you go into work tomorrow, the receptionist tells you that you are a green frog. What nonsense! Then you go to a meeting, and everyone in the meeting tells you that you are a green frog. How absurd! This is obviously a practical joke that your colleagues are all playing. In the evening you go to the theatre, and at the start of the show the compere asks the audience to look around for a green frog. Everyone turns your way. Would you now believe you were a green frog? Probably not, though you might just glance in the mirror. You would still be more likely to believe that it was a practical joke of some kind.

How interesting that when several hundred people tell you that you are a green frog, you are resolute in not believing it. This is because you are retaining your powers of discrimination. Yet when you make a mistake, you label yourself as completely stupid or useless – in other words, you *lose* your powers of discrimination, which would otherwise be telling you that messing up once does not mean you are a idiot.

Think about what you have read in this chapter, and begin to practise this new, enlightening outlook. It will help you develop your self-esteem enormously, as it will give you permission to be fallible and human without feeling a failure. It also establishes that you are not alone, that we are all fallible and make many mistakes in life. This is normality – not the perfectionism that we can wrongly assume should define us.

Other-acceptance

We have now spent some time looking at an idea: accept yourself. Self-acceptance means you don't rely on others to make you feel OK. But there are some circumstances when feed-in from others is positive. This is not denying that we need to be able to create good self-esteem from within ourselves; total reliance on feed-in from others is self-defeating as it means that if we are not getting praise and rewards to back up our own thinking, we lose confidence and retreat to the world of low self-esteem. However, *positive* feed-in from others – other-acceptance – by helping us to discover qualities we may not even know we have, can be valuable for several reasons.

- **It helps you to keep track of how you are doing.** It is an aid, a scorecard. It is input that tallies with our output. It helps us survive low periods when we find it hard to get self-motivated. Someone else paying us a compliment, congratulating us, even just smiling and being friendly, can have a very positive 'lifting' effect.

- **It makes you challenge your Inner Critic.** Other-acceptance is helpful when our own view of ourselves is distorted. We tend to re-evaluate our opinions of ourselves when someone makes a comment that goes against our own thinking. For example, if you are berating yourself for being selfish and thoughtless but a friend says that they always find you very kind and thoughtful, it makes you rethink your own position.

- **It helps you to discover hidden qualities.** Other-acceptance is helpful in offering us insights into positive qualities we possess but may not have been aware of. Qualities are pointed out to you and help you to reassess your view of yourself in a more positive light.

  - ■ 'You always look so nice when you smile.'
  - ■ 'You may not realize it, but your patience has made a real difference to me.'
  - ■ 'How deft you are to do that so quickly.'

Reviewing behaviour

Task

How often in the past week (or longer, if necessary) have you had input from anyone else that was at odds with your worst view of yourself? It might be something as simple as the postman smiling at you or a neighbour waving.

- What negative view might this have challenged? Your view that you are unlikeable? Or that you are not very approachable?
- Write as many instances down as you can think of.

This is a good exercise to do on a regular (perhaps weekly) basis.

Discovering hidden qualities

Other-acceptance helps us to discover positive qualities about ourselves that we were unaware that we had. Glenn Schiraldi (2001) describes an exercise you can undertake with friends to help each of you discover more about your positive qualities. You can do this with just one or two people, but the more the better. It might take a while to arrange, unless you have a houseful of people 'on tap', but do try to set it up, either at work or at home, perhaps over a cup of coffee one day, on the basis that it will benefit all who take part.

Reviewing behaviour

Task

Give each person a pen and a sheet of paper. Put your own name at the top, and then pass the sheet to the person on your right. Each person writes down three things that he/she admires or appreciates about the person named on the sheet of paper, then passes it on to the next person, who does the same. Shiraldi suggests that you scatter your comments around the sheet, so that it is hard to identify who wrote what. Once the lists have been completed by everyone, they are read out – your comments being read out by the person to your left, etc.

When the comments are read out, don't devalue the ones made about you by making deprecating remarks such as 'What are you after?' or 'Obviously no one knows what I'm really like', etc. You will see that the comments are different for everyone, which adds to their value and genuineness. You may not have the same qualities as your best friend, but you both have a lot to feel positive about.

Suggest that everyone keeps the sheet of paper with their name on it. The comments are excellent to refer back to at times when our Inner Critic is on the march and we could use an emotional lift.

This is also an excellent activity for families, especially those with children, who can also suffer from low self-esteem. Children are intrinsically honest and they will be over the moon at receiving positive compliments. A real bond is created between the members of the group.

Accept that you have more qualities than you may be aware of. Many of them are only visible to others, either because you take them for granted or because don't realize how attractive you appear when, for example, you smile or offer to help a friend.

Chapter summary

In this chapter you have learned that:

- accepting yourself is good for your self-esteem
- positive comments by others can boost your self-esteem, as long as feeling good about yourself is not dependent on these
- asking others for positive feed-in can reveal qualities that you did not know you had.

Practise using the skills of self-acceptance, seeing yourself as a complex being with good and bad points, i.e. just the same as everyone else. Remember that what you consider a weakness, someone else might see as an asset (such as having hair a colour that you dislike, or being overly chatty, which you find embarrassing). I hope that you will now be more open to accepting compliments from others, although without becoming dependent on them; don't brush them off with misplaced modesty. Assume that if someone is taking the time to say something nice about you, there is validity to their comment and accept it graciously. Equally, remember that if you appreciate positive comments from others and feel that they raise your self-worth, others will appreciate such compliments about themselves. By raising someone else's self-esteem you will raise your own as you will know that you have done a nice thing.

While self-acceptance is concerned with seeing ourselves as valuable human beings with both strengths and weaknesses, acceptance has a bigger role to play in strengthening our self-belief, walking hand in hand with resilience, covered in Chapter 10.

Acceptance and resilience: the self-esteem partnership

Overview

Chapter 9 looked at accepting ourselves and how this helps us to become calmer and feel better. A further type of acceptance that helps our self-esteem is acceptance of situations. We sometimes hear the phrase 'It is what it is', and where the situation is not a good one it can be hard to believe that you would be able to stay calm about it. But you can. In this instance, acceptance is not a weakness but a strength. It triggers our internal resources to act if we need to, rather than agonize about the whys and wherefores, or what might have been.

However, acceptance, especially in very difficult circumstances, requires a partner and that partner is resilience. These two traits, as you develop them, will become the most important you possess in learning to strengthen your self-belief.

As mentioned earlier, one of the characteristics of low self-esteem is over-sensitivity to externals. If someone makes an adverse comment, we immediately believe they are referring to us. If something goes wrong, we instantly believe that it is our fault. Our brains are over-tuned to absorb comments and events and twist them to mean that we are unlikeable, incompetent, etc. The two key skills in eliminating this over-sensitivity are acceptance and resilience. No matter how much we wish things were different, no matter how many times we go over past mistakes, no matter how often we berate ourselves for not being this or that – things are as they are and we absolutely have to accept that if we are to move forward.

A vital point to make here is that acceptance of ourselves and our circumstances in the present doesn't mean that we should not motivate ourselves to change. Committing to change is vital if you are to achieve strong self-esteem. But you can only do this from the here and now, not from some far off point in the past.

Resilience will help you to make this commitment to change. Resilience, in essence, is the ability to:

- stand firm in the face of adversity
- be able to respond strongly to thoughts, emotions and events that might be upsetting or difficult to deal with.

Resilience will help you to manage your emotional responses and ensure that they are appropriate to the situation you are in.

What is resilience?

When something goes wrong, do you bounce back or do you fall apart? People with resilience harness inner strengths and tend to rebound more quickly from a setback or challenge, whether it's a job loss, an illness or the death of a loved one. To be resilient, you must also be confident – not *in* the outcome but *whatever* the outcome.

By contrast, people who are less resilient – with lower levels of self-esteem – may dwell on problems, feel victimized, become overwhelmed and turn to unhealthy coping mechanisms, such as substance abuse. They may even be more inclined to develop mental health problems. Resilience won't necessarily make your problems go away, but it can give you the ability to see past them, find some enjoyment in life and better handle future stressors. If you aren't as resilient as you'd like, you can teach yourself to become more resilient.

Most readers of this book will have an interest in resilience as part of developing a more self-confident personality. Elsewhere in the world, however, people, especially children, are experiencing lives which, through no fault of their own, are quite horrendous. Civil war, hunger or lack of the most basic resources, such as clean water, require people to survive in the face of enormous difficulties. Resilience in these circumstances can make the difference between death and survival, and so a lot of research is being carried out into resilience, what it means and how it can be fostered and developed. Being able to teach this skill to people will help them immeasurably.

You can benefit from resilience as much as someone in deprived circumstances. While the impetus for resilience research has been primarily to help deprived and disadvantaged people to survive in poor circumstances, what has emerged is an idea of resiliency that is important to emotional good health and is relevant to us all.

Definitions of resiliency by researchers in the field include the following.

- Remaining competent despite exposure to misfortune or stressful events.
- A capacity that allows a person to prevent, minimize or overcome the damaging effects of adversity.
- The capacity some people have to adapt successfully despite exposure to severe stressors.
- The human capacity to face, overcome and even be strengthened by the adversities of life.
- The process of, capacity for, or outcome of successful adaptation despite challenging or threatening circumstances.

Reviewing behaviour

Task

Read the definitions of resilience above.

- Are you able to come up with a definition of your own that would best describe what resilience (or a stronger dose of it) might mean for you? Write it down.

- Think now of any situations or difficulties in your life, either in the present or the recent past, where resilience as you have defined it above would be of help to you. What difference to the outcome might resilience make or have made? Again, write down your thoughts.

The benefits of good resilience

Resilience is the ability to use emotional intelligence to adapt well to stress, adversity, trauma or tragedy. It means that, overall, you remain stable and maintain healthy levels of psychological and physical functioning in the face of disruption or chaos.

- Resilience helps you to cope with temporary disruptions in your life and the challenges they throw up. For instance, you may have a period when you worry about an elderly parent who is sick; resilience ensures that, despite your concerns, you're able to continue with daily tasks and remain generally optimistic about life.
- Good self-esteem is vital in enhancing resilience because it means more than merely trying to weather the storm. It doesn't mean you ignore any negative thoughts and feelings – it means becoming more aware of them, and then being able to deal with them. It does not mean that you always have to be strong and that you can't ask others for support – reaching out to others is a key component of nurturing resilience in yourself.
- Resilience can provide protection against emotional disorders such as depression and anxiety. It helps individuals deal constructively with the after-effects of trauma. Resilience may even help strengthen you against certain physical illnesses, such as heart disease and diabetes.
- People who are resilient have the ability to say to themselves, 'This bad thing has occurred, but I have a choice: I can either dwell on it and beat myself up about it, or I can do something about it.'
- Resilience gives you the skills to endure hardship rather than feel that you are unable to cope.

- Resilient individuals are able to cultivate a sense of acceptance (which is not the same thing as defeatism) and regardless of the setback, they can let go of it and move on.

The characteristics of resilience

The American psychologist and researcher Nancy Davis has identified six areas of competence that she defined as characteristics of resilience.

Area of competence	Characteristics
Physical	Good health Easy temperament
Spiritual	Having faith that one's own life matters Seeing meaning in one's life even in pain and suffering Sense of connection with humanity
Moral	Ability and opportunity to contribute to others Willingness to engage in socially and/or economically useful tasks
Emotional	Ability to identify and control emotions Ability to delay gratification (patience) Realistically high self-esteem Creativity Sense of humour
Social/ relational	Ability to form secure attachments Basic trust Ability and opportunity to actively seek help from others Ability to make and keep good friends Ability to empathize Possession of good other-awareness
Cognitive (thinking skills)	Ability to manage negative thoughts and emotions Good communication skills Openness to a variety of ideas and points of view A capacity to plan Ability to exercise foresight Good problem-solving abilities Ability to take and use initiative Good self-awareness Ability to appreciate and assess the consequences of actions taken

Source: adapted from Davis (1999)

Read through the characteristics in the table above and think about those that may already apply to you, or where they don't yet, whether you could absorb them and develop them yourself.

Here is a test to measure your resiliency – your ability to bounce back from stressful situations. It will test your levels of self-esteem as well as other skills, such as flexibility, creativity and ability to learn from experience.

Self-assessment

Task

Look at each statement below, and rate on a scale from 1 to 5 (where 1 = strongly disagree and 5 = strongly agree) how much you agree with it.

Statement	Rating
I don't allow difficulties to get me down for long.	
I am able to be open about my feelings; I don't harbour grievances and I don't get downhearted easily.	
I am normally confident and possess good self-esteem.	
If things go wrong, I am able to stay calm and work out the best course of action.	
I'm optimistic that any difficulties presented are temporary and I expect to overcome them.	
I usually adapt to changes in circumstances quickly and without fuss.	
My positive emotions are strong enough to help me move on from setbacks.	
I can be quite creative in thinking up solutions to problems.	
I normally trust my intuition and it usually serves me well.	
I am curious, ask questions and I am keen to know how things work.	

I am generally at ease with myself.	
I'm a good problem-solver and enjoy the challenges that problems present.	
I can usually find something to laugh about, even in the direst situations.	
I am able to be self-effacing and laugh at myself.	
I always try to find something positive to learn from my experiences.	
I'm usually good at understanding other people's feelings.	
I am flexible, and can usually adapt fairly quickly to situations as they change.	
I try to look ahead and anticipate and, if possible, deflect problems before they happen.	
I usually consider myself to be strong and independent, and I don't tend to give in when things are difficult.	
I'm open-minded about other people's views and lifestyles.	
I am not constantly anxious when things are uncertain.	
I don't usually fail at tasks I am presented with, provided they are reasonably within my capabilities.	
I regard myself, and believe others regard me, as a good leader.	
I believe that experiencing difficult situations can make me stronger.	
I believe that something good comes out of every bad thing.	

Scores

100–120 You are extremely resilient.

76–99 You normally bounce back quite well.

50–75 You may wobble occasionally.

0-50 You find recovery from difficulties quite hard and you need to develop your personal strength to deal with what life throws at you.

Don't worry if your resilience ratings weren't as high as you'd hoped or expected. It is not hard to develop the qualities that will improve your resilience in all areas of your life.

Improving your resilience

As you read on, make a written note of any of the points that you may need to work on. Keep this to hand as you will use it later in the chapter.

Having checked your score for the task above, what do you think you may need to do to improve your resilience? Write down some ideas.

Practical advice ⇨

Improving resilience

Here are some suggestions for improving your resilience that you may find helpful.

- Look back at other times in your life when you have had to cope with difficulties – perhaps something you felt you would not be able to overcome. What actually happened? What helped you to resolve the situation? Was there anything that didn't help? If so, ensure that you don't repeat that mistake. Building on the way you coped well with previous difficult situations will increase your resilience when you are faced with a new problem. Think also about how you may have changed as a result of dealing with the difficulty. Reflect on this. Are you perhaps stronger than you thought? If you really don't think so – if you feel worse as a result of your experiences – then consider what changes you might make to improve things next time.
- Build strong, positive relationships with your family and friends. These relationships provide mutual support in times of difficulty, which will help your own resilience and help you to offer this to

others. Becoming involved in groups and/or charity work is also helpful. The power of the group, both to nurture you and give you support, is enormous. Groups also ensure that you will never feel alone during tough times.

- Use your thought-challenging skills. Even when things seem dire, constantly ask yourself whether there is a more positive way that you can look at things. If you can encourage yourself to remain hopeful and optimistic when you're in the middle of a crisis, it will be much easier to get through. Resilience is not always about putting things right, but about taking an optimistic view even when you cannot change events.

- When you can, trying to find the funny side of things will always strengthen you – as well as relaxing you in a tense situation. This is sometimes extremely hard, but seeing the funny side doesn't mean you are not taking things seriously – it simply means that when emotions come to the fore, positive emotions will keep you stronger than negative ones. The idea that being angry and distressed is somehow more helpful than being good-humoured is, of course, unfounded.

- Never forget the basics. Your personal ability to develop resilience will depend a great deal on looking after yourself. Make sure that your diet is healthy, you exercise regularly, perhaps practise relaxation exercises or take a yoga class, take care of your appearance and make plenty of time for activities that you enjoy. Nurturing your mind and body in this way will keep you mentally as well as physically strong. Having a sense of personal well-being strengthens your belief that you can tackle difficulties and overcome them.

- Develop the philosophy of acceptance and self-acceptance that we have discussed. Be flexible. Few things stay the same, and it is hard to anticipate the changes that may affect your life, sometimes quite drastically. If you can be open-minded about life events, you will upset yourself less and you will have far more energy to face and, if necessary, tackle change. You will adapt more easily and see the positive side of new events, rather than grieving for what has passed.

- Do something every day that gives you a sense of accomplishment and achievement. This may be something you really don't want to do, but pushing yourself to face up to it and get on with it will strengthen you and make you feel good. Get into a regular habit.

Don't discourage yourself by focusing on tasks that seem unachievable. Instead, ask yourself, 'What's one thing I know I can accomplish today that helps me move in the direction I want to go?'

- With chronic problems, stop wishing and hoping that they will go away, and take some action to put them right. Many of us spend time and energy on simply wishing things would change. Wishing that your problems will go away doesn't usually work and wastes a lot of valuable time when you could be actually doing something about them. Take decisive action rather than detaching yourself from problems and stresses. Once you address your problems with an action plan, you are on the way to overcoming them.

- Learn to be prouder of yourself. Think in positive terms about your abilities and strengths, and mentally encourage yourself to face problems with confidence. Believe you can do it. Positive self-talk is often brushed aside as of little value, but in fact it is a very powerful tool. The more you tell yourself that you are capable and strong, that you can withstand difficulties and criticism, the more control you will have over events and situations in your life and the greater your confidence in your ability to manage them well.

- Everything is relative. Sometimes we see our problems in isolation rather than against the bigger picture of the world around us. This can negatively discourage us as we may see our difficulties as acute and overwhelming. Look around you and evaluate your problems against those of the wider world – and even against those you have weathered before. Once you get a better perspective, your problem will become easier to resolve.

- Consider keeping a personal journal and writing about your deepest thoughts and feelings relating to the events that have happened to you. This can be a very good way of learning to express your emotions, with the bonus of privacy.

- Trying meditation or other more spiritual, rather than practical, ways forward can be of help to some people.

Certain circumstances are impossible to alter, and you cannot change the fact that they have happened and have had an adverse effect on your life. In such circumstances, resilience offers you the chance to respond in the most positive way you can. This may simply be acceptance and forgiveness, or it may be an ability to learn and adapt as best you can. Sometimes, accepting circumstances that cannot be changed can help you to focus on other things that you can alter.

Always remember that something good comes out of every bad thing. You may learn something about yourself that is valuable and positive after a disaster. You may have become stronger through tragedy, or become closer to others who have shared your experience. Resilience grows from facing hardship, and this is a positive result for you. Many people who have faced disaster report a heightened appreciation of life afterwards and a greater sense of joy from simply being alive.

Always focus on solutions, rather than problems. This will give you an active focus, rather than a passive one. Think in solution-focused mode and determine not to dwell on the negative side of the situation.

The most important thing is to identify ways that are likely to work well for you as part of your own personal strategy for fostering resilience. So now write these down.

The three sources of resilience

The International Resilience Project (which is undertaking the resilience research mentioned earlier in this chapter) defines resiliency in terms of three sources, which it labels: 'I have' (social and interpersonal supports), 'I am' (inner strengths) and 'I can' (interpersonal and problem-solving skills).

Look at each of the sources in the box below, and make a note of those strengths that you personally consider to be already present in your life. This will help you discover whether you have, or need to create, the three sources of resilience.

I have …

- people around me who I trust and who love me no matter what.
- people who set limits for me so I know when to stop before there is danger or trouble.
- people who show me how to do things correctly by the way they do things.
- people who want me to learn to do things on my own.
- people who help me when I am sick, in danger or need to learn.

I am …
- a person people can like and love.
- glad to do nice things for others and show my concern.
- respectful of myself and others.
- willing to be responsible for what I do.
- sure things will be all right.

I can …
- talk to others about things that frighten or bother me.
- find ways to solve problems I face.
- control myself when I feel like doing something that is not right or dangerous.
- figure out when it is a good time to talk to someone or to take action.
- find someone to help me when I need to.

For a person to be resilient, he or she needs to have more than one of these strengths. For example, if a child has plenty of self-esteem (I am), but lacks someone they can turn to for support (I have), and does not have the capacity to solve problems (I can), they will not be resilient.

Look at the strengths you have noted down. Are they spread fairly evenly across the three main sources? This would indicate a higher resilience than if they were bunched together under one source.

Resilience as a developing process

Resilience is not a personal attribute because this would imply a fixed and unchanging strength that some have and some do not. It is a more complex process involving internal cognitive (thinking) and personality factors and external protective factors. Resiliency is also a normal, understandable process. It arises from common human qualities such as the ability to solve problems rationally, the capacity to regulate emotion and the ability to form close, supportive ties with others. It is only when these systems are damaged or overwhelmed that natural resiliency fails. In other words, it goes hand in hand with self-esteem. By developing one, you develop the other.

Reviewing behaviour

Task

To develop personal resilience in specific areas, you need to practise.

- Write down four aspects of your life in which you consider yourself to be resilient in general, or to have specifically shown resilience recently. (Use the list you made when we were looking at improving resilience earlier in this chapter.)
- Now do the same for areas of your life where you consider you would like to develop your resilience.
- When you look at the parts of your life where you have shown resilience, what specific attributes have you shown – for example, tenacity, emotional control, ability to see the problem and the solution? Use examples from what you have read so far to give yourself some ideas. Now write them down.
- Look at the areas of your life where you would like to develop your resilience. Would any of the attributes you have identified already help you? If not, what further attributes would you need to develop (again, look for examples in what you have read so far).

How can you develop attributes to help your resilience? Developing resilience means, most importantly, stepping outside your comfort zone. It means being willing to try a little harder, carrying on when you might previously have given up and being willing to feel emotions, such as anxiety and fear, and yet not back down. It also means practice. The only reason most people do not master new skills as well as they would like is that they have not done them often enough for long enough. Keep practising, and the difficult becomes possible, and the possible becomes easy.

The factors in resilience

A combination of factors contributes to resilience. It is not one single attribute, but a process involving:

- internal cognitive and personality factors
- the development of external, helpfully protective factors, such as a supportive family, relationships that create love and trust, provide role models and offer encouragement and reassurance to help bolster your resilience.

Resilience helps your confidence and management of emotions. Several additional factors are associated with resilience, including:

- the capacity to make realistic plans and take steps to carry them out
- a positive view of yourself and confidence in your strengths and abilities
- skills in communication and problem-solving
- the capacity to manage strong feelings and impulses.

All of these are factors that people can develop within themselves. Now think about your personal strategies for building resilience to manage your emotions. Developing resilience is a personal journey.

People do not all react in the same way to traumatic and stressful life events. So when it comes to building resilience, people use varying strategies; an approach that works for one person might not work for another. Some variations may reflect cultural differences, as a person's culture might impact on how they communicate feelings and deal with adversity; for example, whether and how a person connects with significant others, including extended family members and community resources. With growing cultural diversity, we all have access to a greater number of approaches to building resilience.

Think about what being resilient means to you and identify the areas of your life where a more resilient outlook might be helpful in building your self-esteem.

Chapter summary

In this chapter you have learned

- how important the traits of acceptance and resilience are to good self-esteem
- that there are a variety of characteristics present in a resilient personality, and what they are.

Acceptance has often been considered as a weakness but it is, in fact, a great strength. Often, when we value ourselves less than we should, we ruminate about past events where we feel we have performed badly, behaved badly, made bad decisions, 'not seen the wood for the trees', etc. Learning the art of acceptance will change all this. With acceptance we can focus on the here and now and the future. Acceptance doesn't mean we won't attempt to make changes but we do it from the present moment, not from the distant – and unchangeable – past.

You will have recognized that you have some of characteristics of resilience, and others you may have identified and feel that you can now develop. Do persist here. Acceptance and resilience are the qualities which serve us best in our desire to achieve peace of mind and contentment within ourselves as decent human beings.

Now we move to Part 4 of the book: Practice. In this section you will have the chance to develop your self-esteem in certain specific areas, starting with social skills. For many people with low self-esteem, socializing can be difficult, and interacting with others when there is even the smallest smidgeon of conflict can be overwhelming. In Chapter 11 we will look at social confidence and assertiveness, skills that will enable you to engage well with anyone, anywhere.

PART 4

Practice

Keep catching your behaviour and replacing your thoughts each time

Social skills and conflict resolution

Overview

As you have already learned, it is not situations that cause us to become upset with ourselves, it is our interpretations of the meaning of those events. These interpretations define our reactions. How we react, especially when the situation has an element of personal conflict with another person, in turn defines how we view ourselves. Many people simply 'say nothing' because they value themselves so little that they feel they don't have the resources to express their point of view. Others become angry, feeling that this is the only course of action when there is a dispute. This can mean, when someone's self-esteem is low, that even a personal chat with friends can be a strain if someone in the group makes a forceful statement.

Neither of these responses is good for one's self-esteem. Standing down when inside you feel that you should not is often (rightfully) referred to as 'being a doormat'. It is not a relaxed approach but a weak approach. Equally, you will sometimes hear a person say 'I can't bear confrontations'. What they mean is 'I hate losing control of my emotions; my arguments are rarely successful and I end up shaken and upset.'

So we need a way to stand our ground that will not leave us feeling weak or distressed. This is **assertiveness**, which is simple to understand, fairly simple to adopt as a way of dealing with difficult situations, and results in you feeling good about yourself, win or lose (yes, win or lose!)

Many interactive situations don't require a great deal from us other than the ability to hold a reasonable conversation and show interest in others. However, for those with low self-esteem, being in a situation like this can fill them with dread. So this chapter will show you how to mix and mingle in a positive way that will increase your confidence in social situations so that you look forward to such opportunities rather than being concerned about them.

The role of assertiveness in good self-esteem

Does dealing with interpersonal (e.g. social or work-based) situations that might have a degree of conflict in them cause you to feel inadequate? Do you avoid these situations at all costs, feel you are always on the losing end or show yourself in a poor light? Do you currently:

- find yourself getting upset very quickly when others question your opinions and views?
- avoid discussions that might become confrontational, even though it might mean you don't achieve something you need or want?
- say something you then immediately wish you had not said?
- agree with the wishes of others when really you don't agree at all?
- feel your self-esteem constantly dented by your inability to stand up to other people's arguments?

With good self-esteem these thoughts will disappear. Learning assertiveness skills will give you much increased self-confidence. It will also help you to:

- improve your image and credibility
- behave more tactfully
- feel less stressed about confrontation
- achieve desired outcomes in a positive way.

Practice

If you do not already possess these skills, and most people with poor self-esteem do not, then you will need to practise a great deal. This in itself may trigger anxiety in some people, so here is a strategy for making it easier. Learning to deal with daunting situations by planning ahead, rather than relying on instinct, will develop your self-esteem. You can also practise on your own.

Get a voice recorder with a good microphone, and you can practise ahead of time – again and again if you like – without anyone coming back at you to tell you not to be so foolish. We often mentally rehearse what we want to say to someone, so how much better to do it when you can hear how it sounds, and revise it if you need to. Self-criticism in this instance is not another outing for your Inner Critic, but a positive move on your part.

Behaviour changing strategy

Task

Consider a forthcoming situation that you feel nervous about, such as a potentially confrontational discussion with your boss, the builders or a family member. Give some thought ahead of time to what you need to say, and then use a voice recorder to practise.

Listen to how you sound.

- Are you saying too much?
- Or too little?
- Are you sounding too weak
- Or too strident.

Whatever you don't like, note it, and then try again. Do this several times, until you become more confident. Eventually, it will become easy and automatic, and even if you still feel nervous, that will not stop you from saying what you want to say, and in the right way.

Self-assessment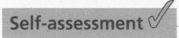

Assertiveness questionnaire

To find out whether you deal with things assertively or not, read through the following statements and give yourself a score for each statement.

Scale: 1 = never, or not like me; 2 = sometimes like me; 3 = always, or very like me.

Statement	Score (1–3)
Section A	
When I have to confront someone about a problem I feel very nervous.	
I am easily upset or intimidated by ridicule or sarcasm.	
Being liked by people is very important to me, no matter what the cost.	
I really don't like conflict and will avoid it any way I can.	
I find it hard to be direct with people if I think they will not like what I have to say.	
Total score for section A	
Section B	
I lose my temper easily.	
I don't care if people like me as long as I get what I want.	
I'll use the tone of my voice or sarcasm to get what I want from other people.	
Patience with people is not one of my strong points.	
I often wag my finger at other people to make my point.	
Total score for section B	

Section C	
I remain calm when faced with sarcasm, ridicule or criticism from others.	
I am not frightened of addressing problems directly without casting blame.	
I am confident about asking for what I want or explaining how I feel.	
I am able to look other people in the eye when dealing with difficult issues.	
I feel confident in my ability to handle confrontational work situations.	
Total score for section C	
Section D	
I often make my point by using sarcasm.	
Rather than speaking out directly to make my feelings known, I'll use impatient or cutting remarks.	
I show my impatience through my body language.	
If asked to do something I don't want to, I'll do it but deliberately won't make any great effort.	
I use silence to make people realize I am upset.	
Total score for section D	

Discovering how assertive you are will help you to spot your weaknesses and make adjustments to get better results and increase your confidence.

What type of person are you?

The questionnaire above is based on identifying which of four different behaviour types you adhere most closely to. The types are:

A – Passive

B – Aggressive

C – Assertive

D – Passive–Aggressive

For which sections did you get the highest scores? You have a clearer idea of where you 'fit' and can identify which behaviour styles most apply to you. You might find that you are a combination of two or three, rather than always acting in the same way.

Now look at Marian's story, and identify the behaviour styles she was using in the various areas of her life – none of which did anything to help her poor self-esteem.

Case study

Marian is 42 years old, married with two teenage children and works part-time in a local office. Her self-esteem is low, and she feels she is neither a good wife, mother or work colleague. At work, she feels over-loaded and unable to keep up with the volume of work coming through to her. Because she has little confidence in her work skills she says nothing, fearful that her inadequacies will be exposed if she says she cannot manage. The problem is that her colleagues have no idea that she is struggling – they keeping passing more work her way, because she 'never says no'. As a result, Marian doesn't enjoy her job at all and is constantly fearful that she may lose it.

At home, her teenagers are fairly noisy, usually untidy and self-centred, emptying the fridge as soon as Marian fills it and spending more time with their friends than on their schoolwork. Again, Marian fears her inadequacies as a mother are to blame for this behaviour. In this instance, however, she tries to remedy the situation by shouting at the children, finding fault with their lazy, noisy ways and punishing them with 'no TV' and curfews when they refuse to toe the line. As a result, her relationship with her children is poor. This convinces Marian even more strongly that she is a bad parent.

When Marian's husband returns from work, Marian feels annoyed that he cannot see how stressed she is and does not appreciate the difficulties she has with the children. Instead of saying anything, Marian remains quiet and a little sulky: 'John should be able to tell how I'm feeling' is her view. Unfortunately, John isn't aware and finds Marian's lack of communication rather hostile. So they spend the evening sitting in different rooms, with no warmth or affection between them at all.

What did you discover? Let's look in more detail at the different behaviour styles that Marian exhibited, and which you may have found that you possess yourself, as a first step to learning how to change them where appropriate. There are four behaviour styles, which can aid or diminish your self-esteem.

Passive behaviour

When we behave passively, we tend to 'let things go'. We may completely disagree with what is going on but don't say anything as we make a negative prediction that things will go against us if we do. If we do speak, we are usually disproportionately deferential, full of premature apology and back down too easily. Being passive is not being relaxed or easy-going; it is being a doormat. This is the behaviour Marian exhibited at work.

Aggressive behaviour

Bully-boy tactics, rudeness, a raised voice, shouting, threats are all geared to ensure that the aggressor gets their way on a 'no matter what' basis. You may have behaved this way yourself on occasion, even if you usually exhibit passivity. For the passive person, never saying what they mean or asking for what they need can eventually lead to emotional overload. Something 'snaps' and suddenly Sally Shy hits the roof and becomes Betty Bully. This is the behaviour Marian exhibited with her children.

Passive–Aggressive behaviour

One of the most common examples of this is the 'silent treatment'. You will know just what that is! You may have used it, been on the receiving end of it or both. Here, we aren't being overtly aggressive (so it's hard to pin anything on us) but we are using silence, sulking, leaving a room when the other person walks in, being deliberately obstructive, etc. to express our feelings. Passive–Aggressive behaviour can also include 'poor me' behaviour: 'I can see I'll have to write that report myself', 'I'm the only one who does anything around here', etc. The objective of this style of behaviour is to get one's own way by making the other party or parties feel guilty. This is the behaviour Marian exhibited with her husband.

Assertive behaviour

The key characteristics of this style of behaviour are that you remain calm and you stand your ground. You are also happy to hear the points of view of others, as you don't feel threatened or intimidated by them. Valid counter-arguments might make you change your point of view, but if not, you clearly stay with what you believe in. You treat others with respect, even if they don't treat you that way. You may be willing to compromise, you speak clearly and you are willing to persist with the discussion until a satisfactory outcome is reached

Reviewing behaviour

Task

Look back over the past week or two, and write down at least one example of when you behaved in each of the four behaviour styles. Most of us vary, rarely using one style the whole time.

Recall how you felt after each event, and rate which felt the best in terms of how you felt about yourself afterwards.

What do you learn from this?

Key skills for assertiveness

When dealing with tricky situations, we can make the mistake of gearing our behaviour to our dominant emotions at the time, rather than to the outcome we wish to achieve. When we behave assertively we focus on outcomes and results rather than emotions.

Before you can behave assertively, you need to *think* assertively. This is because you need to be able to consider the outcomes and results you want ahead of time. These outcomes and results don't just include getting what you want. They should also include:

- how you feel about yourself
- how you feel about the other person
- how he or she feels about you
- whether the outcome you have worked for has improved your relationship for the future, enhanced mutual respect, etc.; in other words, whether it has left your self-esteem in good shape.

Thinking assertively is important because it sets in train the situation–emotions–behaviour–outcome scenario, and it is the point at which you can maintain control and get the situation to work in your favour rather than against you. The work on thought-challenging in earlier chapters is exactly what is needed here. For example:

Situation	A debate with your partner over your holiday destination for next year. Your partner is insisting on a venue you have no interest in.
Your thinking	Rather than feeling upset at the unfairness of your partner's lack of consideration for your views, say to yourself something along the lines of: 'My partner isn't failing to consider me. He/she is just so keen to go to this place that he/she is hoping I might get enthusiastic as well. I'll try and understand what they like so much about it, then express my own reservations, and offer some compromises that fit the bill for both of us as nearly as possible.'
Your emotions	Instead of feeling distressed, you feel OK.
Your behaviour	Assertive. Listening. Acknowledging your partner's enthusiastic preference, while focusing on finding a solution to suit you both.
Outcome	Agreement reached, which might be a compromise venue, or a decision that each of you chooses in alternate years etc. Good relationship maintained. Self-esteem intact.

Behaviour changing strategy

Task

Think of a situation where you will need to use good negotiating skills to achieve the outcome you want. Write down:

- what that outcome is
- using the situation–emotions–behaviour–outcome outline above, write a sentence or two under each heading to show how it might go
- what thinking skills you would use to ensure a good outcome.

Behaving assertively

Once you have mastered these skills, you will be able to:

- confront difficult issues with others
- stay in control of your emotions while you do this
- stand your ground when the going gets tough.

1 Acknowledge the other person's point of view

Most people will expect you to 'come at them' with your own arguments and views, so they will be surprised when you reflect an understanding of their problem. It might be an unrealistic work deadline your boss has imposed on you. An acknowledgement might be: 'The work we are doing is for our biggest client, and I appreciate your concern that we get this project in on time for them.' Acknowledging sets the scene for dialogue, rather than confrontation. You are indicating that you are on the same side as your boss and share his goals.

2 State your own position

Now you have to say where you stand in this situation. If you really cannot meet the deadline, then you must stand your ground on this point. It is often useful to start this step with the words 'however' or 'but', so that you now have: ' … I appreciate your concern that we get this project in on time for them. However, even working solely on this project and nothing else, the timescale is unachievable if we are to produce good work.'

3 Offer a solution

Sometimes an obvious alternative is not readily available. However, remember that this is about results and there has to be a solution, even if it is that the work doesn't get done on time. So your thinking needs to move from 'I can't possibly achieve this' to 'What can we do?' and state the possibilities. Using these steps achieves these vital things.

● It enables mutual understanding of the problems.
● It gives you the respect of the other person.
● It prevents you from being forced to accept an unrealistic/unacceptable/unwanted situation.
● It encourages finding a solution that will suit both parties.
● Your emotions don't get the better of you and cause you to feel upset/angry/disappointed, thus denting your self-esteem.
● The feel-good factor at the outcome is huge, and excellent for confidence building.

Think of behaving assertively as a three-step process and do your best to follow this outline.

Behaviour changing strategy

Task

Think of a situation and practise dealing with it, using the three-step process.

You don't need to wait for a major confrontation; even negotiating over a cup of coffee is a good start and will get you used to the process. You may also wish to practise this with your voice recorder.

Think of the possible responses you might get, and work on how to deal with them assertively.

Being assertive with yourself

Learning to be assertive with yourself is as important as learning to be assertive with others. Look at the case study below and see how the thought processes match exactly with those you need to use when being assertive with someone else.

Case study

Some time ago, I saved a lot of written work on a flash drive and didn't bother to label it. The following day, I decided to save the work again, using a different file name and a different flash drive but again I didn't label it. So now I have *two* unlabelled flash drives. I slipped yesterday's drive back into the drawer (basically, to get rid of it), at the same time thinking, 'You lazy so-and-so. You are making a real mess of your storage. Most people would be prepared to put the time in to clean up their flash drives so that they could just use one and be much more organized.'

Using the model from the previous step, being assertive with oneself might go like this.

- Acknowledgement: 'I appreciate that by putting my file storage back in a drawer without labelling it I am creating a possible muddle for the future.'
- My point of view: 'However, I really cannot be bothered about that right now, and it's hardly a heinous error.'
- Solution: 'If I need a flash drive again in the future, I can just wipe the text off then. I've also got two more unused drives so I may not use it anyway.'
- Net result: Responsibility taken for action. Feeling very relaxed and comfortable having reminded myself that many people do this sort of thing – I'm quite OK.

This is assertive thinking when it applies to you. You have the right to behave however you wish, as long as you take responsibility for it. Most of us sometimes:

- find our fridges full of food beyond its sell-by date (and some of us still eat it)
- have messy drawers we never sort out
- tell white lies when turning down boring invitations
- fail to tidy up the kitchen for days, until we no longer have a single clean plate
- don't ring our mothers enough
- keep the fiver we found on the pavement.

We're fine. We're normal. We are behaving just like everybody else. The key is to accept your own logic and not beat yourself up. Don't get cross with yourself and don't feel ashamed of yourself.

Reviewing behaviour

Task

Write down three issues that you consistently allow to lower your self-esteem, e.g. 'I get very nervous speaking in a group', 'My house is always untidy', 'I'm overweight'.

Now ask at least three (but preferably more, for a bigger sample) family members, friends or colleagues whether they ever suffer from these problems.

What do you conclude from your survey?

Your assertive rights

Thinking assertively means reminding yourself of your basic rights, and then being comfortable with them. Lists of 'rights' can be very long, so we wish merely to remind you of your right to be a normal, fallible human being, and to ensure you appreciate that this makes you just like everybody else and perfectly OK.

You have the right:

- to make mistakes – like every other human being
- to be imperfect – again, like every other human being
- to be in charge of your own thoughts, behaviours and emotions (if these are weird and strange from time to time, you are just like everyone else)
- to tell others what you want and how you feel
- to feel OK about yourself even when you are not on top of things
- to use emotional responses sometimes, even when they are not achieving the right outcome (we all do that more often than we might like to admit)
- to put yourself first sometimes (yes, take that last piece of cake; don't help out if you are too tired; read a book while your partner is cleaning the car)
- to stand up for your rights – or not; it is your choice.

Just remember three things.

1 Rights carry responsibilities. If you chose the right to go to bed late, don't grumble when it is hard to get up in the morning.
2 Others have rights as well. Don't let this deter you from saying your piece, but be prepared for the other person to say theirs too (and that's fine, by the way).
3 See things from the other person's point of view as well as your own.

Behaviour changing strategy

Task

Use the chart below to get comfortable with your rights. Read the example in the first row and then fill in three more 'rights' that you consider important to your self-esteem. Use the thought-challenging columns to counter your concerns with some assertive views.

I have the right to ...	How I view that right with low self-esteem	How to view it with a more assertive viewpoint
Example: Say how I feel.	What I have to say is probably less important than what others have to say. I will be interrupted/ spoken over/ignored.	My views are just as valuable as anyone else's. I will use my assertiveness skills to overcome interruptions and persist with my point of view, while acknowledging what others have to say.
1		
2		
3		

Assertiveness is a key skill for defeating low self-esteem. Having confidence in our ability to stay with an argument, to negotiate with others to reach a mutually satisfying outcome, to stand firm when we don't wish to agree to another's demands: these skills are essential if we are to go into such situations with confidence. As with everything, it is really just a matter of practice. So do go ahead: practise as much as you can, and your confidence will soar.

So far we have talked about the idea that 'being yourself' is important. You need to like who you are and see that you are fine if your self-esteem is to blossom (and remember, this doesn't mean having to be perfect). However, whenever we learn something new, it doesn't come naturally at first, especially in situations that involve us engaging with others. We need the chance to practise first, and this can feel rather like acting, i.e. 'I don't normally behave like this – how can this be normal?' Well, perhaps replacing the word 'acting' with 'practising' will make you feel more comfortable. Yet to start with, it will be acting. Let's look at what this means.

Developing social skills

A good way to improve your self-esteem is to *pretend* to be confident in social situations. Your Inner Critic will encourage you to look at others and point out to you how confidant they are, and how lacking in self-esteem you are in comparison. You are not going to learn now how to check the validity of those thoughts – you have already done a lot of work on that – but how to appear to be just as confident as everyone else; many of them will be 'faking it' successfully, just as you will be.

One advantage of pretending is that after a while we don't have to pretend any more; it becomes natural. We occasionally hear the comment: 'He/she has told that story so many times now that he/she actually believes it'. This is a version of that process. Telling yourself you are confident when you are not is an untruth. But the more you tell it – and, in this case, practise it – the more you will believe it. You will gradually find it easier and easier, and feel less and less self-conscious. So let's start pretending.

Confident body language

When we communicate, over 50 per cent of the message we convey comes from our body language – a form of non-verbal communication. You can therefore send out confident, positive messages without having to say a word.

How would you recognize confidence or lack of confidence from body language? Consider a few ideas of your own, and then look at the list below.

Non-confident body language	Confident body language
Crossing the arms	Open and expansive
Hugging the arms	Good posture
Crossing the legs	Standing asymmetrically
Placing a hand under the chin	Relaxed stance
Stooped posture	Leaning towards the other person
Standing far from the other person	

Use body language to create an impression of confidence. It will make you feel better, even before you have said a word.

- Imagine a string running up through your body and out of the top of your head. Imagine someone pulling this string tight. This will cause you to stand straighter and taller, which always makes you look confident.
- Clasp your hands casually in front of you; don't fold them across your body. You will look more relaxed this way.
- Give a confident first impression by shaking hands firmly with the other person.
- Moderate use of hand gestures can help to convey meaning when you are speaking.

Reviewing behaviour

Task

Practise confident body language in front of the mirror at home.

- Get an idea of how you look using different stances.
- You can also use the 'don'ts' in the list above to see how unconfident you look in these positions.
- If you wish to enlist the help of family or friends, you could ask someone to video you acting out a situation with someone else. This would be particularly useful if you have a special function to attend that is unnerving you.

More 'faking it'

- Cultivate a confident expression – conveying confidence and warmth through your facial expression will make connecting with others much easier.

- Eye contact is an important ingredient of a confident expression but can be hard to get right, especially if you feel nervous – while pretending not to be. Eye contact is important because it shows that you wish to communicate with the other person and are interested in what they have to say. So look people in the eye not only when *you* are speaking, but also when *they* are; this will also help you to gauge their reactions and respond accordingly. Too much eye contact can seem rather aggressive and overpowering; too little can make you seem nervous or embarrassed. A good rule of thumb is to maintain eye contact for about 60–70 per cent of the time.

- Smile! Nothing lights up your face and makes you look more confident than a smile. Not only does smiling (appropriately) make you appear warm and friendly, but research has shown that it will help you to feel more self-confident. Picture someone coming towards you with a warm smile on their face. Nothing could convey 'I'm delighted to see you' more strongly. It is easy to do, and makes a huge difference.

- Adopt a relaxed and friendly expression. This, of course, is often easier said than done, and has to be linked, up to a point, to your basic personality. If you are normally not very expressive, then simply relaxing your facial muscles will have a good effect and will give your face more expression. To assist you, a useful trick is to drop your tongue down in your mouth, so that it touches the base of the inside of your front teeth. Now let the muscles of your mouth curve into a very slight smile. Not only will you look relaxed, hopefully, you will also feel it.

Behaviour changing strategy

Task

- Practise facial expressions in the mirror.
- Say a few words and sentences out loud and be aware of how you look when you say these things.
- Have a go at making statements with a smile (where the content would be appropriate) and see what difference that makes to how you look and how you feel as you say the words. You will find it makes you feel much more confident.

Develop a confident-sounding voice

This is not about what you say, but the way that you say it. Nervousness is audible in the tone of your voice – you may stutter, the pitch may go up or you may speak in a garbled way. When we are anxious about anything our breathing becomes shallow as our heart rate rises. This in turn affects our speaking voice.

Practise controlling your voice and relaxing to reduce anxiety and nervousness.

Slow down! It is better to say nothing than to say so much that it sounds rushed. Become a good listener to increase your confidence in being able to present yourself well without having to say too much.

- Take a few deep breaths to slow your breathing down.
- However nervous you feel, tell yourself that this will pass.
- Allow yourself time to relax before you say too much.

Something else that happens to our voice when we are nervous is that it gets too loud or too soft. Becoming aware of this when you are speaking will help you to adjust your volume. You can also ask family or close friends. Take heed of what they say, and make the necessary changes. A good tip is to exaggerate your mouth and jaw movements very slightly. This will give your vocal chords an opportunity to move more freely.

Another characteristic of nervousness is that we tend to speak too fast. This is less common than speaking too loudly or too softly, but you need to check whether you do this. You can use self-awareness, but it is probably better to ask someone else; in our experience, people are not able to assess for themselves when they are speaking too fast. Recording your voice will not help with this, as you will be working hard to speak correctly. Asking a number of others who you know will be honest with you is the best answer.

Keep the pitch of your voice low. A low, clear voice indicates confidence, but a high voice indicates nervousness. Practise varying the pitch of your voice while speaking into a tape recorder. Listen to authoritative speakers such as newsreaders, and notice when they especially lower their voices.

Work hard on your voice until you feel that it has a confident sound to it – even if you are nervous inside you will appear relaxed.

Behaviour changing strategy

Task

Developing an awareness of how you speak requires lots of practice. Try the following ways.

- Think about your tone of voice when you are in conversation.
- Spend time using your tape recorder – most people are extremely surprised by how they sound. It is not usually what they expected.
- Enlist family and friends if you can, both to comment on your speech in different circumstances, and to role-play conversations with you in the situations in you find it most difficult to come across well.

First impressions

Whatever happens later, the first impression is the most significant factor on which others will assess you – and you them. Think about what happens when you meet someone new. You immediately look for signs and signals that will categorize them in your mind. To project confidence yourself, work on the following.

Dressing appropriately

Don't take the view that how you dress doesn't matter. It may matter to other people, and only an highly confident person (which we assume you are not) would take the view that they really don't care what others think. You *do* want to make a good first impression because it *will* make you feel more confident. So dress appropriately for the situation. If you don't know what that is, don't guess – ask.

One tip here: do give yourself enough time to ensure you look as good as you want to. Nothing is more discouraging to good self-esteem than being in such a rush that you don't have time to change, comb your hair, apply make-up, etc. Look out here for self-sabotage: the old 'I just didn't have time' excuse is often used to explain poor appearance, when the thought process is really more 'What's the point, I'll still look dreadful?' or similar negative thinking. In this case, work on your *thinking* rather than your *excuses*.

Signalling confidence

Ensure that your body language shows the same confidence as your facial expression. During the 'first impressions' stage, you will be judged much more on these things than on what you say. For example, saying 'How nice to be here' while your body language is defensive and your face taut with nerves is not going to carry conviction. People will judge your behaviour more than your comments at this point.

Other points to focus on to make a good first impression include:

- a firm handshake – where appropriate (it isn't always, of course) this indicates excellent self-confidence
- a broad smile – nothing says 'Pleased to meet you' better than this
- good eye contact.

Reviewing behaviour

Task

Think about social or work situations that make you especially nervous. Now consider the last time you were in one of these situations.

- Did you make a conscious, proactive attempt to make a good first impression, or did you just worry about what impression you might be making?
- Replay the situation. What could you have done, or what could you do in future, to ensure that you make a good first impression however you feel inside?

Faking confidence may sound both difficult and insincere. Neither is the case. As with assertiveness, it is all about practice.

- Try 'acting confident' in easy, non-threatening situations at first – just in the local shop, or with the postman or a neighbour. Say a little more than you usually would: focus on your voice and especially on your body language.
- You will soon find that you are no longer acting, and that this is an easy way of being. Thus, what was initially artificial becomes genuine.
- This will give you the confidence to 'act the part' in more difficult situations – perhaps at a party or at work – and literally test out what happens. How do others react to you? How do you feel afterwards? Soon you have a new default and your self-esteem will rise with this.

Chapter summary

In this chapter you have learned that:

- assertiveness is the best behaviour type for dealing with potentially difficult situations

- assertive behaviour enables you to achieve the outcome you want while leaving you feeling good about yourself and maintaining a good relationship with others
- if you start by pretending to feel confident, you start to feel confident
- your body language can make you appear confident even if you don't feel it.

Learning to behave assertively can be life-changing and while you may not yet have acquired these skills you will now understand how superior assertiveness is to other forms of dialogue and actions in potentially difficult situations. Whether you regard yourself as someone who avoids confrontations at all costs or someone who finds managing your emotions very difficult when challenged, learning to stay calm but firm will not only enhance the outcomes you are looking for but will leave you feeling good about yourself and perhaps even proud that you can now handle, with good outcomes, situations that would have led you to distress and self-condemnation previously.

I tend to think of these skills as like a sandwich. The first slice of bread is your acknowledgement of the other person's point of view. The filling tends to begin with 'but' or 'however', as you explain how you see things. The top slice of bread is the solution, which you express if you have one or ask, 'So what's the best thing to do in the circumstances?' if you don't.

Practising this will involve acting at first in a way that is not natural to you. However, the more you practise, the more you will become comfortable with your new way of dealing with things, until it becomes your normal way.

Many people with low self-esteem suffer from poor body image. They are more worried about how they look than what they say, and feel more judged by others for physical weaknesses than they do for what they say or how they present in other ways. If this is a problem for you, Chapter 12 looks at how to deal with it.

Body image

Overview

Poor body image can reduce our self-esteem considerably. Although often thought of as solely a female problem, a lot of men also lack confidence in their looks. Worries of this nature can vary between mild dissatisfaction with their appearance to a problem called Body Dysmorphic Disorder, where people have such a severe problem with the way they *believe* they look that they may resort to unnecessarily severe plastic surgery or become reclusive.

For such people, being unable to come to terms with their physical appearance is the root cause of their low self-esteem. There is a wide spectrum of concern about looks, from feeling unhappy with them but not letting this affect normal life to being so ashamed of perceived flaws that both social and work opportunities are curtailed or completely abandoned.

In this chapter you will learn that your body image has very little to do with what you actually look like, how your body image can affect you and how to get over it.

Is body image a problem?

Finding it difficult to like your looks makes it harder to accept yourself, but you do not need to live this way. You can change your relationship with your body from one of active dislike to one of being relaxed and confident with your looks. First, check whether body image is a problem for you by completing the questionnaire below.

Self-assessment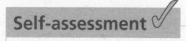

Body image questionnaire

Read each statement and rate your belief in it on a scale from 0 = not at all to 10 = a lot.

Statement	Rating (1–10)
Are you uncomfortable with your body in general?	
Are there aspects of your physical appearance that you really dislike?	
Do you spend a great deal of time worrying about what you look like?	
Do you think that what you look like plays a great part in whether others like you or not?	
Do you think that what you look like plays a part in how much you like yourself?	
When you think of your looks, do the same negative thoughts keep cropping up?	
Do these negative thoughts prevent you from enjoying day-to-day life?	
Do you avoid certain activities or situations (e.g. visiting the gym, going swimming with others) because you feel self-conscious about how you look?	
Are you considering, or have you had, cosmetic surgery for any part of your body?	
Do you depend on clothes and/or cosmetics to try and disguise what you consider weaknesses in your appearance?	
Are you endlessly searching for a new diet, the latest body-shaping exercise, a more flattering hairstyle or dress style?	
Do you spend a lot of time, effort and money attempting to bolster up your imperfect looks?	

Scores:

0–30 Your body image is good; you don't need to read this section of the book.

30–60 Your body image is moderately good, and you are not overly obsessive about it.

60–90 You have a poor body image and spend too much time and effort in worrying about it and trying to change your physical appearance.

90–120 Your poor body image is spoiling your life; you may wish to consider professional help if making changes alone seems too hard.

How did you score? Unless you discovered that your body image is excellent, write down now the aspects of your physical appearance that really bother you. Do you feel that if you looked better it would change how you feel about yourself in general? Note down any ideas you have about how you might deal with this problem.

The effect of poor body image

Many people with low self-esteem also suffer from poor body image. In what ways do you feel that your view of your physical appearance affects your life? For example, do you consider it responsible for you not having a partner, or for your relationship being unhappy?

Self-assessment

Task

Write down the ways in which you consider your perceived physical imperfections affect you.

You may have come up with some of the following.

- My self-esteem is lowered generally.
- It causes much social anxiety, as I feel that others are negatively judging my looks all the time.
- It spoils my sex life, as I hate my partner seeing my body and feel inhibited when love-making.
- I feel depressed about my looks most of the time.

- It has caused me to suffer from eating disorders.
- I never feel really feminine/masculine, so feel less attractive to the opposite sex.

Where have these thoughts come from? A brief answer is … multiple possibilities.

- Perhaps you were brought up by image-critical parents.
- Perhaps you had unusually good-looking siblings who received more praise than you regarding their looks.
- Perhaps you have had a bad experience in an intimate relationship, where a partner you loved and esteemed chose to find fault with your looks.
- Perhaps peer pressure in adolescence or early adulthood to look a certain way or follow trends in fashion magazines caused you to feel unattractive if you did not meet those standards.
- Perhaps you developed friendships with people you perceived to be better-looking than you and who received more attention.
- Perhaps you have a naturally negative way of looking at things which allows you to make interpretations such as: 'I would be better liked if I was better-looking', or 'My looks are holding me back in life'.

Identifying the particular problems that poor body image causes you is the first step to positive change and improving self-esteem. Don't worry about where this has come from – learning to make changes is more important.

Challenging negative beliefs

If you have discovered that you have an extremely poor body image, don't worry. As you now know well, what you think doesn't necessarily have much bearing on reality. Poor body image is based on negative beliefs and assumptions (you remember them from the early part of this book; if not, revisit them) rather than reality. An example of a negative **belief** (a fairly absolute view) in relation to body image could be: 'Good-looking people are more successful in life'. A negative **assumption** (more of an 'If … then' statement) might be 'If I were better-looking, then my life would be much happier'. You can challenge these ideas by finding alternative ways of viewing them, or if your more balanced viewpoint still isn't enough to sway your negative beliefs, you can focus on **evidence** that doesn't support your negative views.

Your goal is to get yourself to rethink, in a positive way, both the assumptions you make about your body image and the importance you attach to it. Once you achieve this, your self-esteem will be in good shape again.

Behaviour changing strategy

Task

Let's look at the belief mentioned above: 'Good-looking people are more successful in life'. Develop some challenges to this belief. How many alternative views can you find? How much evidence can you come up with to disprove this.

Write your answers down, and then check with our suggestions below.

Our challenges to this belief are the following.

- Good looks are very subjective.
- If good looks are the answer to every good thing in life, why do so many good-looking people suffer from depression, broken relationships, etc.?
- Good looks are a temporary asset. People who have relied on them when young find getting older most difficult.
- We get used to people's looks over a period of time, and eventually no longer notice whether they are good-looking or not.

- As many tears are found running down the pretty faces as down the plain ones.
- To many people, looks don't matter at all; that is not the basis on which they judge others.
- Being good-looking often prevents people from bothering to develop the other qualities necessary for a happy life.
- Name some of the most successful/well-liked people in history or in current public life. Were they/are they good-looking?

How many challenges to the belief did you come up with? Does looking at things in a broader and more balanced way help you?

Overcoming negative assumptions

What did you write for your disputing thought in the task above? Perhaps it was along the lines of:

- 'Good looks are nice to have, but they don't account for personal happiness.'
- 'If good looks were all-important, only good-looking people would be happy and successful, yet that is not the case at all.'
- something quite different, but meaningful to you.

Behaviour changing strategy

Task: Challenging negative beliefs about body image

Create a Negative Belief chart like the one below and use it to record your negative beliefs, find evidence that challenges their 'truths' and, most importantly, replace them with more helpful beliefs about your own looks and the place of looks in society in general.

Negative Beliefs chart	
My negative belief about my body image/the importance of good looks in society:	
Evidence that disputes this belief:	
Alternative belief that gives me a more positive view of my body image/the place of physical appearance in society:	
How do I feel about my body image when I look at things this way?	

Note: we don't expect you to undergo a complete change of heart here; that would be unrealistic and unbelievable. But hopefully you will find that you are at the very least starting to loosen your negative beliefs about yourself and to replace them with ideas that are a little more balanced and which make you feel somewhat better. It is important for you to work in this way, as being able to believe a different perception is vital to increasing your self-esteem.

To help you, here are some generic examples of the types of beliefs people with poor body image hold. Some may apply to you, and there may be others that you hold that are not listed here. Use the chart to cover all of them.

- People judge my character by my looks.
- My life would be much happier if I was better-looking.
- I will never be happy until I find a way to change my looks.
- I am physically unattractive and I know other people see me that way as well.
- My [part of body] is too big/too small, etc. and this is to blame for my low self-esteem.
- There is nothing physically attractive about me at all.

> You may have many negative views specific to yourself. Work through them all.
>
> Fill in at least three different negative belief charts, and make a dozen or so copies to use over the next week or so.

If you are agonizing over an aspect of your looks, ask yourself this question: 'What would a starving, homeless person in the developing world say to me if I told him/her that these worries dominated my thinking and prevented me from leading a happy life?' Think about your answer. I am not trying to invalidate your anxieties, which are real and meaningful to you, but simply asking you to place them within the context of other anxieties 'out there', to help you gain a different perspective.

Focusing on the positive

In stories such as *The Beauty and the Beast* or *Cyrano de Bergerac*, the moral of the story is not hard to appreciate. If you also focus less on how you look and more on developing other positive qualities, or appreciating those you already have, others will see beauty in you.

In reality, those of us who worry about our looks are rarely true 'beasts': completely ugly specimens without a saving grace. The problem is, we focus on our perceived weaknesses and worry about them to such an extent that we fail to see any of our positive attributes. The following exercise will correct this distorted focus and encourage you to look at yourself in a more positive light, refocusing on your good points.

Diary/journal write-in

Task

Once a day for a week, write down three physical features that you like about yourself. That's a lot of features! So you'll have to notice the small things, such as the shape of your ears, the size of your wrists, whether you have slim ankles or well-formed toes. What about your knees or the shape of your nose? You can even make perceived negatives into positives; if you are female and worry about having a small bust, think how nice it will be when you are old not to suffer from saggy breasts! This is the level of detail that is required, and you must complete three positive features every day for a week.

My daily diary of attractive features	
Monday	1 2 3
Tuesday	1 2 3
Wednesday	1 2 3
Thursday	1 2 3
Friday	1 2 3
Saturday	1 2 3
Sunday	1 2 3

Repeat this exercise on a weekly basis, i.e. one evening every week, write down three attractive features of your physical appearance. These may eventually be repeats of features you have listed before now but that does not matter. It is the principle of your thinking that will be changing.

> Don't make the mistake of thinking that this is too simplistic to be meaningful. It can be a very powerful exercise, with results that are long-lasting. Be pleased that something so simple can have such a strong effect!

Focusing on the positive may sound obvious, but is not always something we do naturally, and we need to work hard to retrain our minds to work this way more automatically.

Making changes

We are not ignoring the fact that one of the reasons you may have a poor body image is that the reality you see in the mirror is confirming this for you. If you dislike how you look very much, it may be that you do need to consider an appearance adjustment as well as an attitude adjustment.

So why don't you? What's stopping you? We all know the overweight person whose diet 'starts tomorrow' or the unfit person who never visits a gym. The problem here may be that low self-esteem is affecting their effort rating as well. Or it may be that there are hidden benefits in not shaping up, e.g. the excuses it provides for general inadequacy, lack of a relationship, etc.

Ask yourself firmly whether these situations apply to you. Are you failing to acknowledge that there are other areas in your life you need to deal with by using the excuse that your wretched looks are the reason you cannot do so? Think about this and deal with it if necessary.

Monitoring progress

Task

If you really do want to make changes, then we suggest that you set achievable goals (remember goal-setting in Chapter 2?) and work towards them. You can use a chart such as the one below to record these.

Identify your goal in the following way:

- what changes would you like to make to your appearance?
- what physical characteristic do you need to feel better about, e.g. a flabby body?
- what do you need to do to improve this particular physical characteristic, e.g. firm up my physique and lose some weight?

Now break this down into tiny, achievable steps. For instance:

- find out about gym costs and locality
- make a decision about whether to join
- see a trainer about my problems and work out a programme
- ask for dietary advice to accompany the physical workout
- set a time limit for achieving my goal
- set a start date.

Once you get started, record how you are doing at weekly intervals, or whatever time frame suits your goal plan.

Appearance changes I would like to make:	
Physical characteristic I need to feel better about:	
What I need to do to improve this particular physical characteristic:	
Breakdown of steps to achieving this:	
Performance achievements record:	

Using this chart to help you to work out what changes you would like to make and how you could make them is a proactive approach that should result in a feel-good factor from both the effort and the positive results. Simply making the decision to work on these things should prove motivational and inspirational.

Cosmetic surgery

I would neither recommend nor reject this as a possibility for you. I do recommend, however, that you work through the suggestions below before you embark on this course. You may then decide that you feel good enough about yourself not to need surgery after all.

Low self-esteem can lead to 'not bothering' with ourselves, which in turn can lead to poor body image. Make an effort to do all you can to improve your physical appearance.

If you feel no better, you know at least that your problems lie in other, perhaps unexplored areas. You should return to some of the earlier chapters of this book and revisit the skills that will let you dig deeper into some of the more basic beliefs you have about yourself, and work out what is really going on.

Chapter summary

In this chapter you have learned that:

- body image may not be a problem for everyone, but it is unusual for those who suffer from low self-esteem generally to have confidence in their looks
- good looks are not high on the list of qualities that people value in a life partner or a friend
- it helps your self-esteem to address the issues you have with your physical appearance and to do as much as you can to improve it.

When our self-esteem is low, outward appearances can take on real significance. However, not only are physical looks very subjective, they appear well down the list of qualities that people look for in a life partner or friend. A good sense of humour tops most of lists, together with kindness, empathy, intellect and similar life interests. These are also the traits shown to be present in the most enduring of relationships. However, this doesn't mean we should simply 'let ourselves go'. We know when we are doing this and it is important to look for the underlying reasons for this rather than blaming a physical appearance that could probably be improved by a few simple effects.

What you have considered in this chapter may have implications for your perceived ability to achieve and maintain an intimate relationship. As there is much more to having a close and loving relationship with someone than the way you look, we will spend Chapter 13 looking at how you can achieve a close and harmonious relationship and not let low self-esteem spoil things.

Good self-esteem in intimate relationships

Overview

Although low self-esteem manifests itself in a very wide variety of areas of life, outside the workplace the most commonly expressed cause of low self-esteem is in intimate relationships. It seems that, often, our confidence diminishes in an inverse ratio to how much we care for someone. The more we care, the more we wonder what this person could possible see in *us*. These are not cases of unrequited love; many of the clients I work with have partners who love them very dearly and express this. Yet it seems to make little difference. This is because the lack of confidence is within us and our negative thinking can explain every reassurance in pessimistic terms: 'He says he loves me but he probably doesn't mean it'; 'Her work brings her into contact with other chaps she must find more attractive than boring old me'; 'Our relationship will never last. I just can't bring myself to believe that something so good could happen to me.'

In this chapter we'll discuss why finding or keeping a good relationship may be difficult for you. You'll learn confidence-building skills to help improve your relationships and how to hold your head high if a relationship goes wrong. (We should clarify that we are not attempting to simplify the many complex problems that can exist in relationships, but are here focusing solely on issues of low self-esteem and the negative effect it can have.)

The low self-esteem blight on relationships

When we have trouble building or keeping relationships that are important to us, we may feel friendless and isolated, and our self-esteem hits rock bottom. Or is it the reverse? Could it be that it is our low self-esteem that causes us to have these problems? At the bottom of these difficulties lie our own feelings of inadequacy: 'I am not especially loveable/likeable, so why would anyone really care about me?'

Self-assessment

Task

Read the questions below and tick any that apply to you.

Are you in a relationship that you worry about?	
Would you like to be in a relationship, but feel that you don't have enough to offer?	
Do you accept substandard relationships because you feel you are not worth a good one?	
Are you waiting for your partner to 'find you out' and see that you are really not worth loving?	
Do you tend to hold back in relationships so that your partner does not discover all your faults and weakness?	
Do you actively avoid relationships because you cannot conceive of yourself as lovable?	
Do you tend to sabotage perfectly good relationships on the basis that it will all end in tears at some point, so better now than later?	
Do you spoil relationships by being very needy?	

Do you pick arguments simply to rouse your partner to show that he/she 'really cares'?	
Do you feel despondent that you will never feel really loved and content?	

If you ticked even one of those questions, your self-esteem is sabotaging your relationship chances. Confidence in relationships comes only from confidence in ourselves. We need to learn to like ourselves first.

A common problem if our self-esteem is low is that we look for someone else to make us feel better. We decide that if we are liked and loved by others, then we will like and love ourselves. This thinking error is what causes relationships to fail. For if we don't like ourselves, why would we expect others to like us? We need to love ourselves if we want others to love us as well. In relationship terms, this means offering something rather than hoping to take something from a friendship or romance.

In Chapter 11 we discussed being a good listener. The secret of finding and retaining a good relationship is very similar. We need to stop thinking about and worrying about ourselves, and develop more of a focus on others.

Self-assessment ✓

Task

What do you believe prevents you from finding or keeping a happy relationship? Write your answers down.

Do the answers relate more to faults you feel you have that make you unlovable, or do they relate more to faults in most people you meet that make them unlovable?

Gaining confidence in your relationship

Many people say that they have difficulty finding a relationship. This can be because we expect too much of other people, especially if we need them to enhance our self-esteem. They are going to have to be pretty special to be able to do that for us!

To increase your self-esteem, you need to adjust your thinking and practise changing your behaviour. Begin with the following.

Take a real interest in people you meet

This is an excellent skill for gaining self-esteem. Building on the work in the last section, you are basically 'off-focusing'. Instead of thinking about *your*self, *your* needs, *your* inadequacies, you focus on who you are with and ensure you find out about *them*.

This will help you build confidence in your own likeability, and is good practice for relationship building.

Good communication

When we communicate well with our partners or friends, we feel confident and good about ourselves. Poor communication can make us angry and upset or fuel feelings of inadequacy. In your closest relationships it means, yet again, listening well.

When we are in very intimate relationships and no longer on our 'best behaviour', we spend a lot of time either talking or waiting. We are either saying our piece, or waiting for our partner to finish speaking so that we can say our next piece. We don't actively listen.

Understanding

Communicating well with your partner will give you confidence. You will communicate well if you first listen to what they have to say (rather than believing that what you have to say is more important) and then ensuring that you have understood it by commenting in a constructive way.

If Richard tells Alison that he is unhappy about the fact that she doesn't like him spending time in the pub with his friends, she would do better not to respond with a statement – such as 'You obviously prefer being there rather than here with me' – but by understanding what he is saying and expressing how she feels, so that he is given the opportunity to find a solution. For example, 'I appreciate that you like to be able to relax after work with your friends sometimes, but I miss you as well. How can we resolve this?'

Showing interest, and communicating well through listening and understanding will kick start new relationships, enhance those you already have and give you lots of confidence.

Behaviour changing strategy

Task

With everyone you come into contact with today, whether at work, at home or socially, speak less and listen more.

Be aware of the outcomes.

When you do this:

- how do you feel about yourself?
- what is your perception of how others view you?

Just be nice!

How simple is that?! Too simple for you? Look at it this way: one of the difficulties in relationships is our high expectations. The lower our self-esteem, the higher our expectations are. We 'need' our partner to do all the right things, such as:

- to notice if we're unhappy
- to buy the right birthday present
- to spot our new haircut/the weight we have lost.

In other words, we need *them* to make *us* feel good about ourselves.

The result of these demands can be disappointment, and disappointment will confirm our worst fears: we have either made a bad choice of partner, or we are not worth treating lovingly and well.

Where is the focus here? Yes, we're back chasing self-esteem again. Looking to achieve good self-esteem from our partner in our relationship, failing to find it, becoming distressed and feeling worse. We have again become totally self-focused. It's all about *us* again. But, as the sage Anonymous says, 'The secret of a good relationship is not finding the right person, but *being* the right person.'

Behaviour changing strategy

Task

For two days – to start with – stop being needy. This means that you stop seeing things in your terms, and think only about what you can do for your partner.

This is not being a wimp, but an exercise in discovering whether you can actually feel better about yourself by behaving nicely rather than in a needy way.

At the end of the two days, ask yourself the following questions.

- How do I feel about myself and my behaviour (irrespective of the responses I received).
- Do I feel better about myself – have I given my best, even in adverse circumstances?
- Have I noticed any change in my partner? Has he or she appreciated my behaviour, or taken it for granted?
- Would I feel better if I continue to make these efforts?
- How might this affect my self-esteem?

You may say that you have a tricky partner who does not deserve warmth and kindness, and will take you for granted if you behave like this. It is not in the remit of this book to deal with difficult relationships, and you may have to make your own decisions here. I am trying to help you find ways to increase your own self-esteem within your relationship – even if this eventually encourages you to have the confidence to leave a relationship that is bad and unrewarding.

Review your two days of carrying out this task afterwards. Resolve to do a further two days if you can, and then more and more days as you cement your confidence and you get back what you give. Learn to get confidence through kindness rather than neediness. You don't have to get it back all the time in order to feel good. It's OK.

Openness and honesty

When our self-esteem is low, it is easy to sabotage relationships with defeatist behaviour. This can include assuming the worst, focusing on the negative, not allowing yourself to feel exposed in case you get hurt – the type of behaviour that means our partner never gets to know the real person behind the smokescreen.

To succeed in dislodging low self-esteem in *any* area of your life, you need to risk a bit. You need to:

● stretch yourself a little
● change defeatist behaviours
● try something new without being certain of the outcome.

It is no different with intimate relationships. A saying worth remembering is: 'To risk nothing is to risk everything'. Yes, you might get hurt if a relationship goes wrong but you will cope, and can save your energy to deal with that if it happens. Don't waste your energy on it now. You need to risk:

● being open
● speaking from your heart
● letting your partner know the real you.

Reviewing behaviour

Task

Ask yourself: 'With whom do I feel most at ease?'

a someone who tells me only the 'good stuff' about themselves and their life

b someone who is open with me about their faults and weaknesses.

Now consider:

- If I chose a, why?
- If I chose b, do I like them more or less now they have confided in me?
- Do I feel more comfortable with someone who is self-effacing – willing to laugh at themselves and confess their mistakes – or do I prefer someone who never makes mistakes?
- Do I appreciate someone who is willing to confide to me intimate details about their life, or do I prefer not to know?
- Do I actually feel flattered that someone sees me as someone they can tell these things to?
- Based on the above, if I reverse the positions and become the open, honest, intimate-detail risk-taker, is my partner likely to feel more loving and at ease with me, or less?

Remember, to risk nothing is to risk everything. Take a risk with openness and honesty. The boost it will give your confidence to discover how much more you are loved, rather than how much less you are loved, will be well worth it.

Behaviour changing strategy

Task

Each day this week, tell someone close to you – your partner if you have one, your best friend, a colleague – one thing about you that they did not know before.

Be aware of how easy or difficult you found it to tell them, and whether there was any notable response from the person you told.

Build being more open into your daily life until you feel comfortable and confident with this behaviour.

Surviving a break-up with your self-esteem intact

When a relationship ends and it is not of our choosing, it can have a devastating effect on our self-esteem. The pain of losing someone we love is heartbreaking, and any extra pain caused by feelings of worthlessness and unlovability can be extremely hard to bear.

In some cases, people decide never to put themselves through these terrible emotions again. They see the ending as a sign that they are not worthy of being loved and that this is, therefore, how things would end on another occasion.

But while accepting heartbreak, don't allow your self-worth to be called into question. Use your thinking skills. One of the most important skills is not to generalize the specific: this *particular* relationship did not work out; this *particular* person turned out not to be right for you. This does not mean you are unlovable. Use your evidence-finding skills.

- Have you ever been loved before?
- Who else has loved you in your life?
- What does this mean about your lovability?

Behave with dignity. If you can keep your dignity no matter how your heart is breaking, you will keep your self-esteem. Do the following:

- Don't say too much. It is easy to want to pour out invective, go into detail about misunderstandings, how you feel, what happened when, etc. Don't do this: it is too much information, it will not be heard, and it will not make any difference. Say as little as possible, and you will be respected for this – plus, most importantly, you will respect yourself.
- If you still love the person tell them so, but with grace and dignity, and without asking anything in return.
- Determine not to contact them, not to beg or plead or behave in any way that you may regret later and which would cause you more pain and regret. You then increase the likelihood that your lost love will contact you at some point if they hear nothing from you (if that is what you want, of course).
- Be certain that, however much your heart is breaking, you have done nothing wrong and can hold your head up high.
- The difference this type of dignity will make to your self-esteem in the aftermath will be spectacular.

You cannot always keep the person you loved, but you can keep your self-esteem if you act with dignity.

Reviewing behaviour

Task

If you have found yourself in this situation in the past, look back at how you dealt with things.

- What lowered your self-esteem most?
- If it was to do with your own behaviour, what could you learn from that?

Intimate relationships can evoke the highest of emotions. High emotion can overturn rational behaviour and we can find ourselves failing to manage our emotions at all; rather we let them manage us and often live to regret it – and live with the lower self-esteem that can stem from this. If you are in a relationship where you lack confidence or find that this is a 'usual pattern' for you, do reread this chapter and ensure that you understand and then put into practice what you have learned. The difference in your self-esteem and, as a consequence, in the quality of your relationships will surprise you.

Chapter summary

In this chapter you have learned that:

- low self-esteem can prevent us finding and keeping intimate relationships
- refocusing on another person, rather than being wrapped up in our own feelings, makes us both more confident in a relationship and more attractive
- truly listening to someone else is a key skill in any type of relationship
- parting with dignity at the end of a relationship is an important part of dealing with the blow to our self-esteem.

Probably the most important relationship we hope to have as an adult is with a partner for life. Therefore it is important to have enough self-confidence to believe that you can achieve this, and to continue to feel good enough about yourself and your positive contribution to the relationship to maintain it. Each person reading this chapter may be at a different stage in this important life event. However, the skills and 'ways of being' that we have talked about will take you through from a first meeting to lasting love. Overall, it is about considering someone else more than yourself – even if you get nothing back. This is what good self-esteem will enable in you – or to reverse this, if you can behave in this way in a relationship, good self-esteem about the relationship will follow automatically. So do reread this chapter and keep its advice close to hand always. Good luck to you in achieving a healthy and fulfilling intimate relationship.

Next we will look at an adjunct to developing good relationships in all areas and appreciating what you have in your life generally. How optimistic are you? If your self-esteem is low then it's very likely that you are a pessimist. Pessimism seems like a safer place to be. As someone once said to me, 'If I start with the premise that things will go wrong, then I won't be too disappointed when they do.' However, optimism breeds success as it encourages us to risk more, to try harder and to achieve what our pessimistic selves would have us believe is impossible. We therefore take a look at optimism in Chapter 14.

PART 5

Progress

Test your new thought patterns in fresh contexts to progress towards change

Optimism's role in good self-esteem

Overview

If your self-esteem is low, you probably suffer from pessimistic thinking. There are a variety of skills available to adjust this and help you to develop a more balanced view of yourself, others and the world in general, but in essence to have an optimistic outlook is to have a more balanced outlook. This is not about being right or wrong – optimists are not always correct: sticking with the pessimists may be a better option if an optimist urges everyone to jump across a four-foot crevasse. It is simply a thinking style that helps you to take a more relaxed view of life and not to let individual thoughts and events distress you unnecessarily. Being an optimist is a good way to feel about yourself.

Becoming an optimist

Pessimistic thinking reinforces low self-esteem, while optimistic thinking allows us to be more self-accepting and retain a 'feel-good' factor in the face of adversity. Yet the only difference between an optimist and a pessimist is their thinking style. Nothing else. It is largely to do with how we perceive ourselves and events around us, and the interpretations that we give to these perceptions.

For example, if your perception of yourself is that you are dull and uninteresting, your interpretation of possible interactions ('and therefore no one will like me') is what cements your 'feel-bad' factor. We call this **generalizing**, a thinking style you may remember from Chapter 5. So if, for example, you were required to speak to a group of people at work, your generalized view – 'I am so dull and uninteresting as a speaker. No one will have liked the talk I gave' – puts a real damper on how you think you got on. An optimist, however, might say, 'I suspect I came across as rather dull and uninteresting at the group talk yesterday', i.e. the optimist isn't *denying* that he/she may not have spoken well but his/her perception is *specific* rather than *general*. So the optimist's interpretation of that thought is more likely to be 'Some people there may have got a poor impression, but many may not have noticed, and those who know me would not have minded.' So feeling good about yourself has more to do with your view of life than with your circumstances.

You already have the basic skills to become a more optimistic thinker, having learned to recognize and dispute negative (pessimistic) thoughts earlier in the book.

- What do you think about the past?
- Do you consider that it determines your future?
- Do you feel that your genes and your upbringing determined your characteristics and that you are therefore 'stuck with them'?

These types of belief will discourage you from making changes to your life, so take confidence from the fact that change *is* possible and that you will manage it. Neither genes nor upbringing are as powerful as your mind.

Self-assessment ✓

Task

Do you consider that you would feel better if you saw things in a more optimistic light.

Think of two or three events coming up where the outcome is important but uncertain, e.g. a sporting event in which you are competing or an appeal against an unjust parking fine. Being completely honest with yourself, rate on a scale of 1–10 (where 1 = totally pessimistic and 10 = totally optimistic) the thoughts you have about the outcomes.

Event	Rating
1	
2	
3	

Are the ratings fairly consistent?

Does this give you a clue to what type of thinking style you have?

How to think like an optimist

Optimism is good for us. It is a nicer way to be, and the thoughts in our minds from moment to moment are more pleasant. Most importantly, it increases our self-esteem. When we start to think that things might turn out well or that they aren't that bad, we are taking the edge off our negative, self-critical thinking.

Take seriously the need to change your thinking style to one that is more optimistic; if your explanatory style is pessimistic:

● you are far more likely to suffer from depression and low self-esteem
● you are more likely to give up easily in the face of setbacks
● you are less likely to achieve success in the workplace because of lack of belief
● it can affect your physical health, as you will suffer from stress more easily – and life is just less fun.

So how do optimists see things? What is so different? The American psychologist Martin Seligman identified (1998) what he called three 'crucial dimensions' that determine the thinking styles of both pessimists and optimists. These are the three Ps:

- permanence
- pervasiveness
- personalization.

We shall look at these in more detail to ensure that you understand their significance.

Permanence

If you tend to describe bad things that happen using words such as 'always' and 'never', then you have a pessimistic thinking style. To think like an optimist, you need to use instead words like 'sometimes' and 'recently'. In other words, the optimist sees setbacks as temporary, while the pessimist sees them as permanent. Here are some examples that illustrate the point:

Pessimist (permanent)	Optimist (temporary)
I'll never learn to play the piano.	My piano lesson didn't go too well today.
Diets never work.	I'm finding it tough sticking to my diet during the Christmas period.
I'll never succeed in life.	My present job isn't doing me any favours.

The point is this: when something bad happens, many of us feel distressed, even devastated, at that moment. However, for an optimistic thinker the distress reduces and then goes away, sometimes quite quickly. For the pessimist, it stays with him or her, even after only small setbacks; after a major setback, the pessimist may never recover. The thinking style doesn't allow the pessimist to see setbacks as something temporary, from which he or she can recover, as an optimist does. So start thinking like an optimist when you have a setback – describe it to yourself in temporary rather than permanent terms.

The optimistic thinking style for explaining good events is the exact opposite of the thinking style for explaining bad events. An optimist will see good events that happen as permanent; a pessimist will be waiting for them to come to an end. For example:

Pessimist (temporary)	Optimist (permanent)
Good things never last.	There are many good things in my life.
The train is sure to be late today – it's been on time for the last two days running now.	It's great that the trains run on time so often these days.
Life is going too well – something has to go wrong soon.	I love having my life on track at last.

Pervasiveness

Pervasive thinking can cause a poor outcome, as the following case study shows.

Case study

Jane and Tim worked for the same company as graphic designers. When the company lost a major client, it was forced to make redundancies and Jane and Tim both lost their jobs. Although they were both devastated and their self-esteem was dented, Jane recovered far more quickly than Tim and soon found alternative work. Tim, on the other hand, lost interest in everything and put very little effort into applying for new jobs.

These outcomes were due entirely to Jane and Tim's thinking styles.

● When they were made redundant, Jane's view was that her redundancy was a specific event that reflected the company's poor performance at the time.

● Tim's view was that his redundancy reflected his poor abilities as an employee and that he was obviously no good at anything.

When our thinking becomes pervasive, we move from the *specific* to the *all-embracing*. Instead of seeing one error as an isolated incident (as an optimist would), a pessimist sees the error as an indication of total incapability. In other words, he/she generalizes the specific. Here are a few examples:

Pessimist (generalizing)	Optimist (specific)
I'm unattractive.	I'm unattractive to her.
I'm a hopeless driver.	I didn't drive well on the motorway.
Exercise machines are a waste of money.	This exercise machine doesn't perform as I'd hoped.

Behaviour changing strategy

Task

Think about some of the criticisms that your Inner Critic has levelled at you. Write down at least three. Now see if you can write alongside a more specific explanation, using the examples above as a guide.

Criticism	More specific explanation
1	
2	
3	

If you generalize the specific in your thinking, you lose self-esteem in a wide range of areas, rather than just the one area in which events failed to turn out well.

Get into the habit of being far more specific with any criticism of yourself or others. Stop using generalizing statements. This is kinder to yourself, fairer to others, more exact and will help to raise your self-esteem.

Personalization

We discussed the problems of personalization earlier in the book. Blaming ourselves for failure is a pessimist's viewpoint. An optimist will assess what has happened and apportion any blame in a more realistic way. For example, you do badly in an exam. A pessimist is more likely to blame him or herself for being a poor student, and possibly even give up his or her course as a result. An optimist will look at the bigger picture. How could you, thinking as an optimist, view this failure? Write down a few ideas before you read on.

Here are some possibilities.

- The tutor didn't explain things well.
- We had very little time to revise.
- The library was poorly stocked with the books we needed.
- I've heard that many students fail this particular exam.
- I didn't work as hard as I could have done – I'll need to put in more effort in future.
- I do find this subject difficult, but I did my best.

People who blame themselves totally for every failure will have low self-esteem as a consequence. Learning not to personalize events but to look at the bigger picture will help you to think more optimistically and raise your self-esteem.

Note that depersonalization is *not* the same as blaming others. It is taking a realistic look at what has happened, and then considering all the possibilities. As you will see from the example above, the person who failed their exam was willing to shoulder some of the blame ('I didn't work as hard as I could have done') but he/she can also cite other reasons for their failure, as well as thinking constructively ('I'll need to put in more effort in future').

Behaviour changing strategy

Task

Recall the last setback you experienced for which you felt you were partly or wholly to blame. What self-critical thoughts did you have.

Using the example above, write down at least four alternative or mitigating explanations for what happened. This can include your own contribution, but as a part of the whole, not the total.

Self-critical thoughts	Alternative/mitigating explanations
1	
2	
3	
4	

Review how you feel about the incident after you have done this. Is your self-esteem a little stronger from taking this broader view?

If you understand the principles of optimistic thinking and apply the techniques you have learned to challenge negative, pessimistic ideas and assumptions, you will be on your way to becoming an optimist. You will react to the normal setbacks of life much more positively and bounce back from major disasters quickly and well. You will achieve more generally and, most importantly, you will feel good about yourself. Remember, there is no such thing as an optimist with low self-esteem!

Chapter summary

In this chapter you have learned:

- optimism is good for us
- the only difference between an optimist and a pessimist is in their thinking styles
- challenging negative, self-critical thinking creates a more optimistic viewpoint
- the keys to challenging negative thinking are being specific, depersonalizing your view and the three Ps.

Learning to think optimistically requires little more than steadfast practice. It isn't about accurate thinking (it is better to stay with the pessimists if a risk looks bigger than the optimist sees it), it is about seeing things in a way that helps you to depersonalize your views. Personalization is one of three Ps that you need to avoid to achieve a more optimistic outlook and greater self-esteem; the others are permanence and pervasiveness. This is a good chapter to reread as the skills mentioned here are simple enough to implement with only a little practice.

Remember that optimistic thinking is not the same as positive thinking. Positive thoughts can often be incorrect because they require too great a departure from reality in many cases. This can leave you feeling even more pessimistic if your positive thoughts come to nothing. Optimism is more about actively seeing the reality but interpreting it in a way that leaves you feeling better. Do practise this superb skill for lifting your self-esteem.

Sometimes in life we make conscious or unconscious decisions to behave in a way that we are later ashamed of or feel guilty about. Guilt and shame are hard to shake off as they apply to actual events, reactions and behaviours that stay with us and compound our view that we are 'bad' or worthless people. Learning to overcome these difficult emotions is possible, however, and we shall look at that in Chapter 15.

Overcoming guilt and shame

Overview

Low self-esteem is not always just an error of thinking. It can sometimes be caused by a serious error of judgement. Sometimes in our lives we make mistakes that have serious consequences and are hard to live with. The resulting guilt and shame can leave us not knowing how to recover. But we can … and the way to do this is through developing our personal values. Adopting these values will develop you as a person, and a person you will like very much despite the mis-steps of the past or weaknesses in the present.

If we have behaved in a bad or stupid way in the past, this does not mean that we are a bad or stupid person. It is simply evidence that we are fallible. We can learn from such experiences and perhaps become better people in the future through our desire to change our lives.

Case study

Ian worked at an ambulance call centre, responsible for answering incoming calls and prioritizing them so that ambulances were always dispatched to the most serious incidents first. One day, Ian received two calls at the same time that seemed equally serious. However, he only had one ambulance immediately available and he had to make a decision about where to send it. Soon after he made his decision, Ian felt that it had perhaps been the wrong one and became traumatized by this thought. Then Ian discovered that the elderly lady who was the subject of the abortive call had died because the ambulance went to someone else, and he was filled with guilt and remorse because of the choice he had been forced to make. Following this incident, Ian found it harder and harder to continue with the job, and eventually handed in his notice.

Ian kept wondering whether he had made other decisions that had been wrong. His sense of guilt at what he might have done would not leave him and he found it hard to feel good about himself again. Then a friend, concerned for Ian's welfare, suggested that although Ian could not undo the past, he could use his experience to help others in the future. As a result, Ian joined the Samaritans and started to help those who felt they had made poor decisions in their lives and were finding it hard to live with them. This enabled him to make a real contribution to the lives of others. It also helped him to realize that we all make (or believe we may have made) bad decisions sometimes, but that does not mean we are not a person of integrity and value.

Making bad decisions in the past does not prevent us from becoming better people in the future and making meaningful and significant contributions to the lives of ourselves and others.

Self-assessment ✓

Task

Do you suffer from feelings of worthlessness due to past transgressions? Painful though it may be to revisit them, write them down if you can.

Keep them by you as you read on, where you will learn skills to deal with them. (Please do not undertake this task if you think it will be too overwhelming emotionally.)

Recovery from guilt and shame

When bad events happen for which you feel you are to blame, there are three important questions to ask yourself to help you move forward. These are:

● What can I learn from this?

- In what way am I stronger as a result of this experience?
- What can I actively do to make some positive contribution, based on my experience?

There are many examples of people who recover their self-esteem by acknowledging and accepting what they have done as a human failing, forgiving themselves, and then using that experience to become stronger and possibly to actively help others. Don't just dwell on past misdemeanours and let your Inner Critic hound you. Use positive activity, forgiveness and self-acceptance as skills to create or restore your self-esteem.

Positive activity

Think of the number of reformed drug addicts who lecture in schools and colleges, telling their own stories and attempting to inspire young people to better lives; people who have misused alcohol and lecture on the evils of drink; even murderers who go on to reform and live useful lives. Ask yourself: 'If I cannot put this right, how can I at least create some good from it?' This might be through simply being open with others about your past behaviour and the consequences of it for you, so that they have an opportunity to learn not to take the same path.

Forgiveness

Forgiving yourself is just as important as forgiving others. You need to work on both of these aspects of forgiveness together. How can you forgive yourself if you cannot forgive others? Equally, as you learn to forgive others, why can you not learn to forgive yourself as well?

Self-acceptance

Self-acceptance is powerful because it does not rely on us being good in order to feel good about ourselves. Be kind to yourself and strive to do better, to move forward positively – but accept your past imperfections as being normal human frailty, rather than making you a terrible human being. Self-acceptance also means being honest with others about yourself. If you are ashamed to talk about your fallibilities, how can you learn to accept them? There is often the bonus that others do not judge you nearly as harshly as you judge yourself, and you learn to see things in a different light.

The ghost of past experiences

Low self-esteem can be the result of childhood experiences, and where these have been especially traumatic, low self-esteem may be very deep-seated. You have become used to being strongly judgemental of yourself – and this can overspill into being strongly judgemental of others as well. How do you overcome this?

In the same way that a person who misuses alcohol may need to stop drinking completely, your own way forward is to stop judging – completely. You must stop evaluating both yourself and others as being good or bad, right or wrong. This will require a great deal of willpower and commitment, but the rewards will be enormous. As you stop judging others, you will stop judging yourself. You will come to learn that we cannot quantify good or bad, right or wrong. Our views are almost always subjective, and learning acceptance of them will be empowering.

Here are some examples of what you could do.

- You could give up moral judgement of the behaviour of others. This will be hard, especially in some circumstances, but you could start by saying to yourself that they are making what they see to be the best choice of behaviour available, according to their own needs and values at the time.
- When you read newspapers or watch television news programmes, stop yourself from automatically making an instant 'right or wrong' judgement.
- Stop rating both yourself and others as being better/worse than anyone else. Simply accept people as unique individuals.
- Stop using critical descriptions, such as 'selfish', 'stupid', 'ugly', 'lazy', etc.

- Stop blaming anyone else for your own negative feelings and unhappiness.
- Stop judging yourself in any way; this includes your thoughts and your behaviours. Accept yourself as a fallible but OK human being.

Behaviour changing strategy

Task

This is an on-going exercise. On a weekly basis, select one person you know whom you don't especially like.

- Consider what specific aspects about them you don't like and write these down. Now spend some time going over these aspects in your mind and rewrite them in a non-judgemental way.
- If you have contact with this person, practise being pleasant and non-judgemental towards them. Most importantly, be aware of how they treat you in return, and how you feel afterwards.

Negative thoughts give you valuable information

If you still suffer from a variety of negative thoughts and emotions, don't worry. These are giving you valuable information about the areas in which you can make changes. If you feel gloomy and sad, then you need to focus on developing the value of cheerfulness. If life seems flat and dreary, then you can learn to build passion into your life. If you feel inadequate and unable to achieve your goals, then some determination will make a difference.

Finding true happiness

Over the years, much research has been undertaken by psychologists world-wide to pinpoint the most important values we, as human beings, may either have or need to develop in order to feel truly happy and contented. Some of those get flagged up again and again as making a huge difference to people's lives.

Making a contribution

If you can consistently develop the idea of contributing to others' well-being, the sense of pride and self-esteem you feel will be more than any accumulation of wealth, celebrity or accomplishment can ever give.

Professor Martin Seligman undertook a research project in which he gave a class of students an assignment that involved doing one altruistic act and one pleasurable act every day for a week (Seligman, 2002). He asked them to rate the 'feel-good factor' that they got from both these things. He discovered that:

- at the start of the exercise, the feel-good factor for both the altruistic and the pleasurable acts was similar
- the week after the exercise, the feel-good factor for the altruistic acts remained far higher than that for the pleasurable acts.

Not only does altruism raise your self-esteem, but the positive feelings will stay with you rather than fade away. Developing core values that help you to feel good about yourself will ensure that your self-esteem becomes healthy and enduring.

Diary/journal write-in

Task

Undertake Professor Seligman's experiment, either at work or at home. For one week ensure that you do one pleasurable act and one altruistic act on a daily basis.

Rate the 'feel-good' factor on a scale of 1–10, where 1 = OK and 10 = very high. Note down your ratings on the day, then a week later revisit them and rerate the feel-good factors. Which acts still give you the highest rating?

	Altruistic act	Pleasurable act	Rating on day	Rating a week later
Monday				
Tuesday				
Wednesday				
Thursday				
Friday				
Saturday				
Sunday				

What values are important to you?

What are the values that guide your life? Are there values you wish you had but don't feel that you possess? If not, why not? Write a list of the core values that are meaningful to you, and which you consider would enhance your self-esteem.

A good way of working out the values that are important to you is to pick someone whom you admire for their character (rather than their skills or abilities) and write down what qualities you consider them to possess that make them an admirable person.

Your self-esteem will grow enormously if you select which of these attributes are important to you and make a real effort to develop them and to incorporate them into your life.

Determination

This is an attribute that you must possess or develop if you are going to create lasting self-esteem for yourself. Determination is the quality that will help you to meet challenges and overcome setbacks. It is what will make the difference between feeling stuck and moving forwards powerfully and confidently.

Love and warmth

You can develop these qualities by using many of the skills you have already worked on – most importantly, by focusing on others rather than yourself. Stop seeing everything as being about you and become genuinely interested in and caring of other people and their problems and situations. Ask yourself what you could do to help, even if it is nothing more than listening or being available. Don't always respond to anger with anger – see if you can melt the anger by responding with warmth and compassion. This isn't weakness; it is strength (and, therefore, quite hard to do).

Appreciation and gratitude

Take a moment to stop thinking about what you want that you don't have, and think instead about what you do have. Concentrate on appreciating all the good things that have come into your life, the helpful things that people have done for you and the joy of what you have achieved. You will enhance your life greatly by thinking in this more appreciative way.

Forgiveness

When we fail to forgive people, we are the ones who remain disturbed and upset and let this affect other areas of our lives. Taking a 'why should I?/how could they?' approach is all very well, but you are the one who will remain resentful and bitter. How does this help you? Forgiving is what allows us to move on. It inspires respect from others and gives us self-respect. It is worth working on.

Humour and cheerfulness

These are very visible qualities. Is this necessary? Yes, it is. Being happy within yourself but not sharing it with others is only half of a good thing. Being overtly cheerful will make the people around you happier as well. Think of it this way. When things are tough, does not being cheerful make things any better?

Humility and integrity

See yourself as neither inferior nor superior to anyone else. Treat others in the same way – have respect for the simple person; don't be in awe of the powerful person. Use your best endeavours at all times without looking for praise or reward.

Excitement, passion and vitality

These are qualities you can actually bring into your life quietly. They don't have to involve being a noisy extrovert, bubbling with ideas (although they can). Rather, they encourage you to think proactively and get moving! You cannot be excited and passionate if you are slumped in a chair listening to your Inner Critic running you down.

Flexibility

Flexibility as a value? Yes, it is one that will almost guarantee feeling good. Consider the thinking skills you have learned. These could also be called 'learning to think flexibly'. Or, 'if your approach isn't working, change your approach'. Being flexible is about being willing to change your rules for living, your assumptions, the personal meaning you attach to things and your actions. Throughout your life there will be aspects in it that you are not able to control, so adopting a flexible approach to the meaning of these things will enable you to feel good about yourself.

Self-assessment ✓

Task

Read through this chapter again. Then undertake a self-audit to identify which, if any, of these qualities you think you already have.

If you have not already written them down, do so now. Then rate each quality with a percentage (where 0% = not at all and 100% = totally) according to how strongly you believe you already possess them.

Quality	Rating (%)
Determination	
Love and warmth	
Appreciation and gratitude	
Forgiveness	
Humour and cheerfulness	
Humility and integrity	
Excitement, passion and vitality	
Flexibility	

Rating is important to allow you to develop further the qualities you already possess and to measure future improvement.

If you do your best to incorporate these values into your daily life, your feel-good factor will rise up off the chart. Your life will flourish, and you will reach your highest potential.

Working on your values

We hope that you now have an idea of the personal values that you would like to improve or possess. Within the scope of this book we cannot work in detail with you on each of these values, but we can help you to develop a plan that you can work on yourself on an on-going basis.

We also suggest that you consider reading in further depth about these values. See the Further reading section of the book for suggestions. Each of these books discusses in depth the acquisition of the core values that have been identified throughout history, across nationhood and different religious beliefs, to be those that bring us lasting happiness and good self-esteem.

Monitoring progress

Task: Creating your personal plan

Now it is time to start developing a personal plan using the goal-setting suggestions in Chapter 2. You can build on it over days, weeks and months in order to enhance your own core values and/or help you to master new ones.

Look at the overview of your qualities that you created in the last task. Select one or two qualities that you feel would be the easiest to start with, and/or have special importance to you.

Consider whether you possess elements of these values at present, and list them. Rate how strongly you possess each value with a percentage, where 0% = not at all and 100% = totally.

Now set your personal plan and timescale, which we suggest you make four weeks. This will give you time to notice a real improvement in your self-esteem but it is not so long a period that you will give up.

After working on these values for four weeks, consider how your present values have improved and what new values you now possess. Rate again how strongly you possess each value with a percentage, where 0% = not at all and 100% = totally.

Consider whether you need to do further work, e.g. do you need to record how you are doing for a further four weeks? Are there certain opportunities you're not taking? Do you care more about some values than others.

Developing values: My personal plan

Value(s) to develop/develop further:

_____

_____

_____

_____

Elements of these values I possess now (with strength rating in %):

_____

_____

_____

Improvement in present values after four weeks (with strength rating in %):

_____

_____

_____

New values I now possess (with strength rating in %):

_____

_____

_____

What further work, if any, is needed?

_____

_____

_____

Work on one new value at a time. In week 2 you can build in a second value while continuing with the first, and in week 3, a third value, and so on.

After four weeks, you may find that the values are beginning to become second nature. If you are still struggling, then continue with this exercise for a further four weeks, or as long as it takes for you to feel that they are a natural part of you.

Feel free to make changes as you go along. You will only be able to measure your improved feel-good factor as you try out new behaviours. Some things may surprise you, e.g. you might start doing more for others reluctantly, only to discover that your feel-good rating is much higher than you had predicted. Or you may set great store by being flexible, but find that unless you are careful you are 'giving in' too easily. Redefine your values in the light of what you discover as you work on them.

This is a very positive exercise for increasing your self-esteem. All you are working on is increasing the good qualities that are within you but which need to come to the fore. You should find this both pleasurable and rewarding and begin to feel much better about the very valuable and unique person you are.

Chapter summary

This chapter has taken you through what we might call the 'final process' of raising your self-esteem. You have spent the previous chapters learning a variety of skills which are valuable in 'normalizing' your sense of self. This last chapter has taken you one step further – to be the best person you can be while accepting the fallibility in all of us. 'Normality' isn't perfection; it is a balance between being partly great, partly average and partly 'not as good as we could be'. It is about accepting yourself, liking yourself, acknowledging your weaknesses while striving to improve in areas that are important to you. All this makes you the totally likeable, totally fallible, occasionally brilliant person that is you.

Bear this in mind. You can achieve whatever you wish if you know exactly and specifically what you want, you have the skills to achieve it, and you have a plan: and the most important part of your plan is *action*. You can write as much as you like, in as much detail as you like, on as many sheets of paper as you like, but action – actually doing something – is the only thing that will make a difference. Becoming active is the key to good self-esteem. You can do it! I wish you the richer, better and more confident life you will deserve as you achieve success through your efforts. My hope for you is that you will become pleased to be *you*.

Appendix A: When going it alone is too hard

Where problems of low self-esteem are chronic and deep-seated and you have tried your hardest to eliminate these difficulties on your own without complete success, you might wish to consider professional assistance.

Psychological therapy can be extremely helpful in this regard. In this book, we have used what is called a 'solution-focused' approach – cognitive behavioural therapy. If this approach appeals to you, you might wish to work with this type of therapist.

Insight-based (psychodynamic) therapy will explore your past, looking for unresolved unconscious conflicts that are holding you back in the present.

Some therapy is described as 'integrative'. Here, the therapist will draw on different orientations to suit the client and/or the problem at different points in the therapy.

Life coaching can also be useful if you feel stuck in a rut, as it is a very goal-oriented and motivational approach.

Your first port of call may be your GP as he/she will know what psychological services are available to you on the NHS and privately. You will probably have to wait for treatment on the NHS, while private therapy will be available at short notice. If you take the private route, ask your GP to recommend local therapists.

The following websites provide access to some of the organizations you can contact directly to find a therapist in the United Kingdom. Be sure to check that the therapist is professionally accredited to the organization you contact.

British Association for Counselling and Psychotherapy
www.bacp.co.uk

British Association for Behavioural and Cognitive Psychotherapies
www.babcp.org.uk
United Kingdom Council for Psychotherapy
www.ukcp.org.uk
Association for Coaching
www.associationforcoaching.com
Centre for Coaching
www.centreforcoaching.com
Centre for Stress Management
www.managingstress.com

Contacting the author

I hope you have enjoyed reading this book and have benefited from the challenging activities within it. If you wish to contact me directly, you can do so by emailing me at: chrissyw2@aol.com

Appendix B: Low self-esteem and abuse

The two areas of low self-esteem dealt with below can be complex problems, and as such it is beyond the remit of this book to deal with them in depth. However, we wish to highlight them, and some of the resources available to anyone who is struggling with them.

Low self-esteem and alcohol

For many of us, a drink or two to calm our nerves before a difficult meeting, a daunting social situation or just to relax can be beneficial. However, using it as a prop to disguise the real problem – lack of confidence and low self-esteem – can cause people to become alcohol dependent. They begin to make the erroneous connection that they can *only* cope if they have a drink.

We should stress that you must be brutally honest with yourself about any alcohol dependency. While improving your self-esteem may reduce your reliance on alcohol, it is addictive. You may find it too difficult to stop on your own.

If you want to reduce your alcohol intake but would like help to do so, we suggest that you read one of the following books or contact Alcoholics Anonymous. Do not wait until you have a really serious problem to do this. Nip it in the bud.

Books
Bert Pluymen, *The Thinking Person's Guide to Sobriety*. If you are dithering over whether or not you have a problem, this book will help you decide.
Allen Carr, *Allen Carr's Easy Way to Control Alcohol*.

Websites
www.smartrecovery.co.uk

Low self-esteem and abusive relationships

Many people – usually women, but sometimes men – stay in relationships that are verbally abusive and/or physically violent because their self-esteem is so low that they lack the confidence to leave. These destructive relationships can range from occasional outbursts to regular violence. If you are in an abusive relationship and wonder if you should leave – or know you should, but lack the confidence to do so – you can seek help. We suggest some resources below.

Books

Mira Kirshenbaum, *Too Good to Leave, Too Bad to Stay: A step-by-step guide to help you decide whether to stay in or get out of your relationship.*

Patricia Evans, *The Verbally Abusive Relationship: How to recognize it and how to respond.*

Dawn Bradley Berry, *The Domestic Violence Sourcebook*. This includes practical steps for leaving a violent relationship.

Website

www.nationaldomesticviolencehelpline.org.uk

References

Anthony, R., *The Ultimate Secrets of Total Self-confidence* (San Diego, CA: New Thought Publications, 1979).

Beck, A. T., Rush, A. J., Shaw, B. F. and Emery, G., *Cognitive Therapy of Depression* (New York: Guilford Press, 1979)

Davis, N. J., Resilience Working Paper: Status of the Research and Research-based Programs (1999), http://mentalhealth.samhsa.gov/schoolviolence/5-28Resilience.asp

Schiraldi, G., *The Self-Esteem Workbook* (Oakland, CA: New Harbinger, 2001).

Seligman, M., *Authentic Happiness* (London: Simon & Schuster, 2002).

Seligman, M., *Learned Optimism* (New York: Knopf, 1991).

Further reading etc

Brandon, N., *Six Pillars of Self-Esteem* (New York: Bantam, 1994).

Bunch, M., *Creating Confidence* (London: Kogan Page, 1999).

Burns, D., *10 Steps to Great Self-Esteem* (London: Vermilion, 1993).

Burns, D., *The Feeling Good Handbook* (New York: Penguin, 1999).

Canfield, J., Hansen, M. and Hewitt, L., *The Power of Focus* (London: Vermilion, 2000).

Carr, A., *Positive Psychology* (Hove: Routledge, 2004).

Cash, T., *The Body Image Workbook* (Oakland, CA: New Harbinger, 1995).

Covey, S.R., *The Seven Habits of Highly Successful People* (New York: Simon & Schuster, 1989).

HH The Dalai Lama and Cutler, H.C., *The Art of Happiness: A handbook for living* (London: Hodder & Stoughton, 1998).

Davies, P., *Increasing Confidence* (London: Dorling Kindersley, 2003).

Fennell, M., *Overcoming Low Self-Esteem* (London: Constable & Robinson, 1999).

Gawain, S., *Creative Visualization* (Novato, CA: New World Library, 1995).

Gillen, T., *Assertiveness* (London: CIPD, 1998).

Hauck, P., *How To Be Your Own Best Friend* (London: Sheldon Press, 2002).

Laurence, T., *You Can Change Your Life* (London: Hodder Mobius, 2003).

McKay, M. and Fanning, P., *Self-Esteem* (Oakland, CA: New Harbinger, 2003).

Padesky C. and Greenberger, D., *Mind Over Mood* (New York: Guilford, 1995).

Palmer, S., 'Self-acceptance: concept, techniques and interventions', *The Rational Emotive Behaviour Therapist* (1997), 5.1, pp.3–30.

Perry, M., *Confidence Booster Workout* (London: Hamlyn, 2003).

Robbins, A., *Awaken The Giant Within* (London: Simon & Schuster, 2002).

Webber, C., *Get The Self-Esteem Habit* (London: Hodder & Stoughton, 2002).

Young, J., *Reinventing Your Life* (New York: Penguin, 1993).

Mindfulness resources

'Simply Being' app

Kabat-Zinn, J., *Mindfulness for Beginners* (2 CD set)

Index